EDUCATION OF A GAY SOUL

Education of a Gay Soul

Nicholas F. Benton

BCI Books, Inc.
Falls Church, Virginia

Published by BCI Books, Falls Church, VA, May 1, 2021

Book design and layout by Toby Johnson and Nick Gatz
Copyediting by Tami Nelson

Cover by Nick Gatz

ISBN-13: 978-0-578-90958-5

EDUCATION OF A GAY SOUL

Contents

Preface   9

Introduction   13

1 What is Gay Sensibility?   19

2 Arrival of an Amoral Sensibility   57

3 The Science of Same-Sex Orientation   77

4 The Modern Movement   91

PHOTOS   113

5 Conceived in the Shadow of
   Tennessee Williams   117

6 American Roots   135

7 Gay Science   168

8 Gay Jesus?   179

9 Prometheans   197

Index   215

About the Author   227

Preface

Being gay is about something more
profound than our sexual nature...There is a
kind of flagrant joy about us that goes very deep
and is not available to most people.

—Paul Monette

In the fall of 2010, a years-long gathering storm of creativity finally erupted in my mind, leading to a swift and powerful output of columns on the subject I called "Nick Benton's Gay Science" that carried on weekly for two years in a popular Washington, D.C. gay magazine, *Metro Weekly*. I threw everything I had into them, recalling, reading, researching more than at any time in my life before to produce exactly 100 original 800-word essays. They dealt with the subject of what it means to be gay from a myriad standpoints. I read back on them now and am still amazed at them.

They took the form of an argument against the prevailing male dominated, hedonistic-centered culture that has defined what it means to be gay in a twisted and wrong way. Most of the establishment gay community has bought into it because it crafts gay identity in terms most favorable to it. It is time, as I have argued since my activism in the earliest days of the post-Stonewall gay movement, for gays to define themselves on their own terms and not those of the dominant culture. To put it succinctly, my studies found that we as gay people correspond best to the ancient Greek archetype of the Promethean life-giving model, not today's dominant archetypal Dionysian pleasure-seeking model. It is time to begin shaping a new gay identity and culture based on this discovery. We are not conformists with this dominant culture, or enemies who define ourselves against it. We are constructive non-conformists whose role is to shepherd society to a better place.

A year after I was spent at the "Gay Science" essays effort, I found a publisher willing to reprint them all in the form of a book. Steve Berman at the Lethe Press gave it the go ahead and a talented editor turned them into book form, all 100 essays in order. That was published under the title, *Extraordinary Hearts: Reclaiming Gay Sensibility's Central Role in the Progress of Civilization.* Three times it rose to Number One in the Amazon rankings of "Gay Studies" books. Between then and now, I gathered and published a volume, *Gay Men in the Feminist Revolution: Articles, Pamphlets and Reflections on My Gay Activist Days in San Francisco, 1969-1972,* a collection of articles and essays I knew would be of interest to a much smaller circle of scholarly interest but something I felt needed to fill in blanks in the historical record of the movement.

Also in the meantime, I've continued to publish my own general interest weekly newspaper inside the Washington, D.C. Beltway. I founded The *Falls Church News-Press* in 1991 and we have just completed 30 years of consecutive weekly editions (over some 1,560 weeks). I routinely contribute some 4,000 words to each edition, including an editorial and national affairs column.

My "Gay Science" columns of 2010 to 2012 were over and above all that, and what I've decided to do with this volume is to take them all and try to sort them out in a more rational order to represent as a more coherent argument. I've asked my talented friend Toby Johnson, who'd been that editor/ book designer at Lethe for the original collection, to help me with this and he has done an exceptional job.

—Nicholas F. Benton,
Falls Church, Virginia,
April 2, 2021.

Introduction

THE COVER OF THE APRIL 8, 1933 *Saturday Evening Post* by artist Norman Rockwell showed a farm boy standing in a field listening intently as a life-sized fairy in a green dress whispers in his ear—the artist's stealth affirmation of a boy's gay awakening. That awakening, we can see in retrospect, was an indispensable precursor to the late 1960's eruption of the modern gay movement. And it wasn't just the awakening of that single boy or that beloved and influential illustrator. It was the awakening of a cultural and artistic sensibility that would change the world and change the souls of so many men and women who had discovered themselves to be homosexual.

Growing up as a gay lad myself in the post-World War II period, I never met a self-identified gay person until I was in my mid-20s. Liberace notwithstanding, I'd never knowingly seen one on TV or in a magazine, either.

Born February 9, 1944, a few months before D-Day, I grew up in a California coastal town of 50,000 north of Los Angeles. My gay awakening came more than two decades after Rockwell's representation of the green fairy. I knew I was different from my earliest days as my interests took me to places unfamiliar to my family: my interest in newspapers, the U.S. presidents whose names I memorized, classical music, and my special empathy toward my struggling, abused mother. At the onset of my adolescence, I developed a special relationship with another boy my age. For a year-and-a-half, we were famously inseparable, taking long bike rides, founding a junior high newspaper (that I recruited him into), and sleeping over at each other's homes.

As a result of the Kinsey reports about sexuality published in the late 1940s, the term homosexual began being used outside professional circles for the first time in the 1950s. One night my brother asked about the term at our dinner table and I felt my face burn with an intense blush. The same thing happened later in a college classroom when someone asked about the movie version of

' play, *Suddenly Last Summer*, and our teacher made a disparaging comment about homosexuals.

I loathed my gayness. Whenever the notion was suggested it was in an overwhelmingly negative way. Acting it out was simply not an option. I vowed to take my secret to the grave. If five to seven percent of the species is naturally born with a gay sensibility then from the dawn of civilization and all around the globe, imagine how many have faced similar conditions like mine in my youth, but for their entire lives.

The silence began to be broken very slowly with the emergence of modern electronic mass media: radio, movies, and TV. Coded representations were permitted rarely with allegories usually involving spunky misfits battling tyranny. J.M. Barrie's *Peter Pan* smashed stuffy British convention with the depiction of a leader among homeless boys aided by a fairy. Barrie's Peter maintained his youth and puckishness by contrast to the "normal" boys he rescued, who in the final chapter are followed into their boring, mediocre, "normal" adulthoods.

Misfits also conquered evil in the classic *The Wizard of Oz* with Dorothy played by a young Judy Garland. She later became a wounded misfit in her own right, thereby a gay icon. Gays adopted the term "Friends of Dorothy" as a coded reference to their kind. Women in the movies and on TV who struggled to break the mold of the straight, white male-dominated culture resisted conventionality with their strength. Suffering consequence, they became champions to those of gay sensibility, the likes of Bette Davis, Joan Crawford, Marilyn Monroe, Katharine Hepburn, and Lucille Ball.

As an adolescent gay boy, I was swooning to the songs of a gay Tab Hunter, gay Johnny Mathis, gay Tommy Kirk (the young star in *Old Yeller*), a pajama-gaming gay Rock Hudson, gay James Dean, and gay Sal Mineo. Little did I know, and not find out for many years, that two hours away, my aunt was renting her house to the creator of *Cabaret*, the famous gay writer Christopher Isherwood and his young gay partner, Don Bachardy.

Mimi Swartz' article in the June 19, 2011 *New York Times Magazine*, "Living the Good Lie: Should Therapists Help God-Fearing Gay People Stay in the Closet" followed by an "ex-gay's" chronicle, seem to miss completely the most fundamental point about what "coming out" means to most gay persons. Being "in the closet" for the person who is conscious of an erotic attraction to others of his or her own sex is not really about hiding a secret or "giving up any opportunity to have fulfilling relationships as gay men or women," as Swartz contends. It is about something more personal and important shall we say, to the soul. The "closet" has most essentially to do with denying integrity, perhaps the most important quality to a healthy, productive human being.

I was a seminary student when I came out of the closet, just preceding the 1969 Stonewall Riots. It was a life-changing decision made in the midst of a world in turmoil, anti-Vietnam War demonstrations, civil rights marches, and ferment in the ghettos with the assassinations of monumental leaders for constructive change, Dr. Martin Luther King and Bobby Kennedy.

It was a decision to claim my own life, to rip it free from the cruel conventions of an unjust society that threatened the most severe punishments if I did not live a lie. I had been forced to be two-faced, duplicitous, lying, deceptive, and untruthful on a basic level to all those around me, including those I cared for the most.

The social ferment for justice and equality caused me to realize that, as Dr. King said about African-Americans, I could not be leaned on if I refused to stoop over. So, I decided to stand up.

It was the most important thing I've ever done. My relationship with the gay world has been a spotty one at best, including what I considered extensive periods of virtual exile while the irrepressible surge of radical hedonism in the 1970s set the stage for the AIDS epidemic.

But once I stood up by coming out, it compelled me immediately to devote whatever talents I had to build the gay liberation movement so that my experience could be shared by as many others as possible. More importantly, it provided me with a personal strength through the new-found integrity of my inner soul to throw off the accumulated burdens suffered through years of emotional and physical submission to the whims of a tyrannical father.

My father died in 2002 and toward the end of his life we became close and I respected, loved, and helped him despite everything. After all, he'd passed onto me certain strengths of character that not only gave me the courage to come out but also to confront him at the risk of violence when I had to.

It was Christmas Eve 1970, and when I arrived by bus from San Francisco to our family home on the Southern California coast. I had long hair and a beard and my father didn't need to know anything more than that. He dictated that I would not be welcome at the family dinner, even though my two brothers, their wives, and my grandparents would be there. It was a long day leading up to the dinner. My brothers and their wives debated in the living room about whether or not to boycott the meal in my defense and bemoaned our shared lives of putting up with our father's arbitrary, violent, and tyrannical ways for so many years. But in the end, they all decided to cave in and show up, leaving me isolated and excluded.

I decided I could not allow that to be the final word, even though my father's physical strength was legendary and he had a history of inflicting pain on my mom and us boys. I knew if I confronted him he could pulverize me. I opened the front door to my parents' house to find everyone at the dinner table. Upon seeing me, they froze with forks and knives in hand and looked at me speechlessly with stunned, wide-open eyes. I assumed a pose as one steeled for a fight and unleashed a stream of loud, angry invectives against my father. When I was spent, I was surprised my father had made no move toward me. He continued to sit and sputtered, "So, you want to ruin our dinner?" I turned on my heels and strode out, slamming the door. As I walked away, not my father but my brothers chased after me threatening me for my violation of their shameful compact of subservience that they knew was wrong.

I viewed that night as sealing my coming out, claiming my integrity and my life, and freeing me to become whatever life had in store. Never again would I cow-tow to unreasonable convention or fear.

1

What is Gay Sensibility?

IN THIS BOOK, I AM EXAMINING the prospect that there is something unique and defining that underlies the fact that a certain number of us turn out to be homosexual, and not heterosexual. In other words, where does homosexual orientation come from? If it is not from a deficiency or sheer randomness, then what?

By unique I don't mean superior. Gays (shorthand for LGBTQ+ people) are different from straight people and therefore by that obvious fact unique. What is at the core of that? If it can be found, wouldn't that help to define a positive identity for gay people, generally? When I suggest that three aspects help to define gay identity – notions of sensibility, an alternative perspective, and constructive non-conformity – I do not mean that these qualities are unique to gays. On the contrary. What is unique is gay sensibility, gay alternative perspective, and gay constructive non-conformity.

I do not claim to impose an identity onto gays, obviously, I couldn't if I wanted to. I strive to raise questions and propose hypotheses out of which a more universal sense of gay identity may emerge, if not immediately, perhaps over decades or longer.

At present, that identity is not defined. Society's definition of homosexuals as a class of persons is barely 150 years old, although there is an abundance of documentation of same-sex relations going back as far as historical records have existed. Up until the word homosexual was first coined in 1859, persons in same-sex relations were defined individually by their behavior solely, either punished, reviled or in some rare cases grudgingly tolerated. Homosexuals as a class of persons is a very new concept emerging with the rise of urban cities and the transport and communication means for their explosive growth following the industrial revolution. The notion of a gay community had become possible for the first time, just as the telephone had a revolutionary effect on urban culture 100 years ago and as the Internet has now.

ASK SOCRATES

THROUGHOUT HISTORY, HOMOSEXUALS HAVE EXPRESSED THEIR unique natures, not through sexual orientation but far more prominently through sensual perspective. The unique sensual perspective of homosexuals has informed our poetry, art, music, governance, scientific method, and sympathies for the downtrodden and oppressed throughout history. Our rock-star founder, the homosexual Socrates (by way of Plato) is perhaps the most influential thinker and inventor of the scientific method in the history of western civilization. He spoke about the dual realities of sensual perspective and sexual appetite in Plato's works most directly addressing homosexuality: *The Symposium* and *Phaedrus*.

In particular, in the second speech of *Phaedrus*, the allegory of the charioteer and his two conflicting horses Socrates articulated what he called "the science of love". The soul is composed of its winged charioteer and of the two horses, one is good and one is not. The first: "The horse that is harnessed on the senior side is up-right and clean-limbed; he holds his neck high, and has a somewhat hooked nose; his color is white, with black eyes; his thirst for honor is tempered by restraint and modesty; he is a friend of genuine renown and needs no whip, but is driven simply by the word of command." The second: "The other horse is crooked, lumbering, ill-made; stiff-necked, short-throated, snub-nosed; his coat is black and his eyes a bloodshot gray; wantonness and boastfulness are his companions, and he is hairy-eared and deaf, hardly controllable even with a whip and goad."

So, said Socrates, "When the charioteer sees the vision of the loved one so that a sensation of warmth spreads from him over the whole soul and he begins to feel an itching and the stings of desire" the two horses act in an entirely different way. While the white horse and charioteer are "constrained by a sense of shame" the black horse "utterly heedless now of the driver's whip and goad, rushes forward, prancing, and to the great discomfiture of his yoke-fellow and the charioteer, drives them to approach the lad and make mention of the sweetness of physical love."

Socrates continued the allegory: "At first the two indignantly resist the idea of being forced into such a monstrous wrong-doing, but finally when they can get no peace, they yield to the impossibility of the bad horse and agree to what he bids. So, they draw near, and the vision of the beloved dazzles their eyes. When the driver beholds it the sight awakens in him the memory of absolute beauty...and in so doing inevitably tugs the reigns so violently that he brings both horses down upon their haunches; the good horse gives way willingly and does not struggle, but the lustful horse resists with all his strength."

Socrates demonstrated that by the charioteer's ability to restrain the "lustful horse" he was able to honor the beloved and his beauty with true and enduring love. Socrates was pointing toward the kind of gay sensibility I have identified as he contrasted "excellence" to "pleasure" as the foundation of love.

The post-Stonewall gay movement has had the black horse as its core paradigm. The challenge for our future is in our ability to start consciously pulling on its reins. This vision of the loved one as an exemplar of excellence corresponds with my own childhood experience and those of countless other homosexuals I have talked with and read about over the years. Though it is not what the popular media—including the gay media—generally portrays as homosexuality.

That difference is what I call a gay sensibility and it is more pervasive for one's personality than sexual orientation, usually preceding it. This, and not sexual orientation alone, is the central defining feature of homosexuals. From a scientific perspective, gay sensibility shows up routinely in human societies as dominant among a minority of persons. Indeed, it is an outgrowth of nature's creative process that has dissymmetry, not symmetry, as its core. Since symmetry or equilibrium leads to stasis it cannot account for the dynamic unfolding of creation. So, there must be a basic dissymmetric element to creation which energizes a binary universe to grow, expand and develop. In philosophical terms, it is analogous to the active communicating component of a dialectic form of reasoning that advances knowledge. The binary system of human species development is the distinction between its male (testosterone-based) and female (estrogen-based) components. But this system requires a dynamic bridge element to progress, and this element is comparable to the notion of gay sentiment. It is the component that tempers the otherwise stark distinction between the pure male and pure female parts, allowing for nurture and growth, fending off the extremes of dominance and submission otherwise inherent. It is a vital, indispensable component of creation itself.

Therefore, the person who finds him or herself to harbor a rich, defining portion of gay sensibility actually bears a special role in creation, and as such is the bearer of a special gift not only in terms of one's own identity but to society, as a whole.

Gay sensibility is a special gift. It is a gift that cannot be returned, as much as many may wish it could. It can be squandered, erased, or destroyed, but remains a natural gift nonetheless.

We with a gay sensibility are not only capable of loving and caring for persons of our own sex in ways that those without it can't match, but we also have a unique capacity to love and care for persons of the opposite sex, because we do not measure such persons from the standpoint of dominion, procreation and society's structures for perpetuating these. gay sensibility empowers us with a unique capacity to love all persons regardless of gender, in a compassionate, empathetic way.

Naturally, such sentiments become co-mingled with the complex mysteries of erotic arousal but for the self-actualized person, while these are powerful, legitimate, and drive a longing for reciprocal romantic relationships they do not overwhelm a positive sense of personhood to fundamentally interfere with the creative vocations pursued to put a gay sentiment to best use in the world. Surely, the pressure to conform exists for everyone in society, straight or gay. Gays have good reasons to conform, with reasons ranging from reassuring everyone we're non-threatening and enjoying a sense of security derived from conformity to the unresolved, residual post-traumatic stress syndrome of the AIDS Dark Age. But homosexuals are simply not wired for conformity.

CONSTRUCTIVE NONCONFORMITY

HOMOSEXUALS CAN'T BE CONFORMISTS WITHOUT TRYING very hard and are never quite up to the task. A passion to conform is almost as bad as being in the closet. It is just not natural. All the empirical evidence suggests that homosexuality pertains to the whole psyche of the person and not just to the narrow aspect associated with sexuality *per se*. An often-profound sense of differences in childhood tied to different interests and desires is normative and amplified as erotic arousal manifests itself to present two related, naturally-generated realities for homosexuals. The first I describe as gay sensibility and the second as a different sensual perspective. These two factors operative in homosexuals establish that we look at the world in a fundamentally different way from non-homosexuals. Walking into a candy store, ninety percent of the people gravitate toward a certain favorite and evaluate and prioritize everything in the store from that standpoint. The ten percent who prefer a different favorite accordingly look at everything differently. What is natural is for homosexuals is what I call "constructive nonconformity." It could also be called "creative" or "compassionate" non-conformity, but "constructive" is preferred because it derives best from the notions of gay sensibility and sensual perspective and also defines natural gay non-conformity against corruptions of that concept.

To be specific, "constructive nonconformity" is not the kind of anarchistic, self-obsessed, destructive, and power-centered notions of non-conformity defined by the Beat Generation and related radical hedonist currents that hijacked the gay movement in the aftermath of Stonewall. It is not the post-modernist ugliness exemplified by the theories and mandates of the French deconstructionist, nihilistic philosopher Michel Foucault. Nor is it the so-called "queer theory" current that worships Foucault as some sort of saint and thereby embraces his jaded, angry, and cynical perspective on reality and behavior. No, "constructive nonconformity" reflects the enduring contributions of many homosexuals in history. While they can be awesomely camp and outrageous as in the likes of a Liberace, *The Birdcage* movie heroes, or figure skater Johnny Weir, such nonconformists are constructive, life-affirming givers of love and compassion as was the remarkably nonconformist life of Eleanor Roosevelt.

Imagine Eleanor Roosevelt breaking from every convention by simultaneously redefining the accepted definitions of both a First Lady and of a woman in general. She guided her physically-disabled husband through the nation's most trying times of depression and war and emerged after his death to champion the most progressive achievement of the modern era, the Declaration of the International Rights of Man. Most historians declared her husband FDR the Man of the Century for the 20th century. I give it to her, hands down the Person of the Century. And she was one of us.

Conformity is the bane of our or any age. In our times, young people are tracked almost like chattel into social expectations that lock them with few variations into routinely mundane and mediocre lives to reinforce the powers that be. Not a totalitarian system, this is the norm for our democracy and it is done through the vast resources of social engineering by our ruling class.

Boys play sports to prepare themselves to fight and die in wars. Girls play with dolls and cheer boys on the sidelines of sporting events, groomed to comfort the fighting men and have their babies. Alternatively, today's young are groomed to attend college, become steeped in student loan debt, find a job to pay it off, afford marriage, buy a house, and have children. By their early twenties, they're set in cement, locked in at an early age with few inspired or motivated to buck the trend.

Televised sports, fantasy sports, sophomoric soap operas, and other cultural drivel preoccupy them leaving little time for anything original and creative. Meanwhile, American society drifts relentlessly to the right, toward indifference to the poor and paranoid about everything beyond its borders. So much for conformity.

It takes constructive nonconformists to alter such patterns for the betterment of us all, both by working individually with persons and with society as a whole. That means us.

HORRIFY DESPOTS

> "The attitude of great poets is to cheer up
> slaves and horrify despots."
> —Walt Whitman, *Leaves of Grass* (1855).

THIS QUOTE HAS BEEN FRAMED AND posted on the wall in front of my computer in the *Falls Church News-Press* office for years now. It is the most succinct statement of everything I stand for and what my newspaper is dedicated to. That's of little wonder when you consider the source. It is hardly irrelevant that the author hailed as perhaps the greatest American poet ever is "one of us." I contend that for a variety of reasons Walt Whitman's notion of the "great poet" in his incredibly influential *Leaves of Grass* published in 1855 represents a high watermark for defining the positive notions of gay sensibility alternative sensual perspective, and constructive non-conformity that I have articulated as platforms for a new gay identity.

Whitman, who was certainly what we'd call gay today, coined the term, "great poet" to describe sensibilities that are commensurate with the exercise of democracy in the young American republic and are entirely coherent with gay sensibility as I've described it, and as I've discovered most LGBT people to have experienced it in their own lives. He coined the term at least fifteen years before social psychologists invented the word homosexual. Contrasted to existing labels laden with negative connotations in use in his time, Whitman carved out a universal notion of the "great poet" who stands staunchly for equality of all persons, on the side of the plight of the working poor and the oppressed, and for the merits of science, invention, beauty, sensuality, art, and reason to lift humanity towards a better place.

Leaves of Grass in its early editions was condemned by many because it was considered immoral. Its sensual and homoerotic content leaped out from its pages, especially in its "calamus poetry" section. But while many students of same-sex history view this as a precursor of an emerging homosexual subculture in the U.S., *Leaves of Grass* as a whole defies such narrow identity pigeonholing. That was Whitman's point.

The "great poet" has command over the whole world by bringing the unique and passionate alternate perspective that drives constructive nonconformity toward equality, democracy, and justice. Thus, Whitman's 27-page *Leaves of Grass* introduction has a universal expression of gay sensibility dripping from its pages. By this definition, the sensibility that precedes erotic arousal in homosexuals drives them toward an embrace of the talents and professions that correspond to Whitman's articulation of the "great poet."

That's really who we are. The same-sex part is a subordinate but defining component. It is a signpost that we are that element of nature that drives it from what was to what will be, from stagnation or regression toward progress defined by expanding democracy, science, education, and art. It is not defined by the inward-turning, narrow, calcified categorical thinking that sees reality in rigid terms of heterosexual and homosexual, and organizes humanity in defense of one or the other. When everyone is fighting for their gains and homosexuals become inclined to seek only their rights all are thereby susceptible to becoming stingy and indifferent to the plight of others.

The "great poet" of Whitman inclines strongly for equal justice for all under the law, regardless of anything about orientations, sexual, or otherwise. Therefore striving for the full legal and cultural enfranchisement of homosexuals is a worthy and meritorious undertaking. However, the "great poet" does not advocate this to the exclusion of the full enfranchisement of all persons, including the poorest and most needy. While the massive influence of Whitman's *Leaves of Grass* on the psyche of all Americans in the latter half of the 19th century, through its many editions, additions, and edits, until and beyond Whitman's death in 1892, its impact was especially profound in the burgeoning American cities where the networks of creative and compassionate self-identified homosexuals grew quickly to something that persisted through ebbs and flows into the late 1960s, as described in George Chauncey's *Gay New York, 1890-1940* (1995), and Nan Alamilla Boyd's *Wide Open Town: A History of Queer San Francisco to 1965* (2003).

That was the world into which came still only the tiniest fraction of the seven percent of all humanity that inclines to homosexuality which took me 24 years to first discover in San Francisco. America's greatest poet, the gay Walt Whitman provided us with our core gay identity 150 years ago with his notion of the "great poet," combining it with a passion to "cheer up slaves and horrify despots" and touting the virtues of democracy in his epochal work. The "great poet" was inseparable from the felling of tyrants and the promotion of the disenfranchised through the promotion of mighty institutions of righteousness and democracy. This notion of gay sensibility is fully compatible with, indeed, a very spirit of our noble United States of America. Sorry, right-wingers, America is, at its core, very gay.

DAVID, ALEXANDER, AND ABRAHAM

IN THE MANY MODERN HISTORIES OF homosexuality, studies document evidence of same-sex sexual behavior, dating back to the boundaries of pre-history, without making serious distinctions between same-sex relations defined by faithfulness and commitment to common virtues, and those which were exploitative, depersonalizing, predatory and destructive. For example, in ancient Rome, the widely-accepted practice of male prostitution, on the streets and in the temples, legal and taxed by the state until the sixth century A.D., is reported in the same value-neutral breath as citations of sustained commitments to mentoring involving older-younger pairings, or long-term relations among equals. It can be argued that the entire Judeo-Christian tradition and certain currents of most other major religions, it is the contrast between love, nurturing and the shared values of virtue, respect for persons and justice, on one hand, and against brute force, lust, rape, and might-makes-right behaviors, on the other hand, which is at the core of their ethical structures.

Taken in this light concerning same-sex relations the Judeo-Christian tradition condemns the behavior of the rapes of Sodom and Gomorrah and the lustful practice of male prostitution in the Roman Empire (the Book of Romans) and yet holds up as exemplary a long-standing love affair between two males, David and Jonathan, as virtuous and worthy not only of being recorded but maintained over eons as the Books of Samuel in the Biblical canon. In like manner it can be argued that the entire tradition is built around the essential content in the famous prose poem of the Apostle Paul, I Corinthians 13 expounding on the qualities of love. With no reference to deity or doctrine this chapter stands alone, a mirror of similar praises of love in Plato's *Symposium*, above gender and sex and their traditional roles in a patriarchal society, as if the original anthem for homosexuals who are called to liberate and advance societies beyond their myriad forms of slavery and barbarism. Every creation by someone who is homosexual is by its very nature gay, including every great work of Williams, Walt Whitman, Oscar Wilde, Christopher Isherwood, Cole Porter, and the list goes on.

Dating back to the earliest times of recorded history, great poets and intimate same-sex affection have been associated with the conquest of tyrants and the establishment of virtuous governments. The first and most famous case is that of the young David who slew Goliath in the Old Testament. David was more than just a prototypical underdog he was destined to become one of the greatest poets in history (author of most of the Old Testament Psalms), the subject of the longest account of an intimate interpersonal relationship in the entire Bible involving Jonathan, for whom his love "passed the love of women," and the great king of a righteous people.

"Your love to me was wonderful, passing the love of women," David said of Jonathan at Jonathan's funeral (2 Samuel 1:27), following earlier Biblical accounts of the two exchanging clothing, embracing, weeping together, hugging, and kissing each other.

Based on the notion of gay sensibility, it is not necessary to prove the nature of this relationship by deducing that there must have been explicit sex between the two. No, here is gay sensibility explicitly and deliberately reported by the author of 1 and 2 Samuel and preserved in the Old Testament, presented as a key element for understanding David, inclusive of his tyrant-slaying, poetry, and nation-building. Sorry, right-wingers, the Bible is at its core, very gay.

As with the ancient Greek city-states, the correlation of gay sensibility with the construct of just, democratic institutions of government emerged again in the Renaissance when the image and spirit of David became the signature of Renaissance culture David, as the slayer of tyrants, was adopted by the Florentines as the patron and protector of their democracy. The first large freestanding statue in 1,000 years was of a bronze David, crafted by Donatello. With the head of Goliath under his boot and sword, in this famous statue young David appears as a downright "flamer" sporting a fey hat and an angelic face. Later alternatives to Donatello's rendering by Verrocchio and Michelangelo (the most famous one) did away with the swish and presented a more conventional hero.

When America's Founding Fathers grappled with how to construct an enduring union based on certain "inalienable rights" extending to all persons, they had few precedents to rely upon but the works of the ancient Greeks, including the great homosexual Socrates and the extensive pro-homosexual symposiums and dialogues in which he took part. One of the most eloquent apologists for Greek models of democracy, law, and justice and author of at least 51 of the 85 Federalist Papers in the earliest days of the American republic was Founding Father Alexander Hamilton. It is well known to Hamiltonian scholars and historians the intense, intimate relationship between the young, brilliant Hamilton and John Laurens (i.e. Ron Chernow, *Alexander Hamilton*, 2004). "I wish, my Dear Laurens, it m(ight) be in my power, by action rather than words, (to) convince you that I love you," a young Hamilton (born in 1755 or 1757) wrote in one of many affectionate correspondences with his contemporary in George Washington's revolutionary army in the 1779-82 period before Laurens' premature death in a military foray in August 1782.

Hamilton had it very rough being born and growing up in the British West Indies, his father deserting his mother and leaving him branded as a bastard (all his life, actually), then becoming orphaned and a virtual street urchin at age 14. An older patron recognized his brilliance, however, and sponsored him and turned his life around. At 17, Hamilton, described as "bookish, delicate and frail," published his first poem in a newspaper in St. Croix. An articulate author and brilliant thinker, once in the colonies, he was recruited at age 20 by Washington to be his aide-de-camp in the revolution.

His relationship with Laurens, who was born to a high station in South Carolina, was based on their shared, passionate anti-slavery, abolitionist sentiments. For Hamilton, his sensibility for the downtrodden extended to the Jews, for whom he had the greatest admiration. Little doubt why he and Laurens stood so firmly against the tyrant King George III determined to topple him on behalf of universal human rights.

The progression in America's development from the gay sensibilities of Founding Father Alexander Hamilton to the next great gay American leader, Abraham Lincoln, is astonishing for the common vision and approach they took advancing the cause to, in Whitman's words, "cheer up slaves and horrify despots." Hamilton's profound, romantic affection for John Laurens has not awaited modern homosexual studies to be recognized. In her 1902 biography of Hamilton entitled *The Conqueror: Being the True and Romantic Story of Alexander Hamilton*, Gertrude Atherton wrote that the bond between Hamilton and Laurens "was romantic and chivalrous. Each burned to prove the strength of his affection, to sacrifice himself for the other."

While Hamilton died at the hand of an assassin, technically in a duel with Aaron Burr at age 47, his indispensable achievements in the forging and providing for the sustainability of the great American experiment in Constitutional democracy were achieved against seemingly overwhelming parochial sentiments that would have made the young nation easy pickings for the British to rend it asunder with divide and conquer tactics. Therefore, Hamilton's passionate desire to establish a strong central government and a national bank to direct its defense and development was born of his staunch determination to forge a lasting bulwark against tyranny.

Despite his premature death in 1804, his institutions and their merits outlived him and were bridged to Lincoln by the great Whig leader Henry Clay. Clay's passion was also to prevent the dissolution of the union, and that mantle was passed to Lincoln who then could only prevent its division by prosecuting the Civil War. In his monumental study *The Intimate World of Abraham Lincoln* (2005), the late C. A. Tripp surveyed four of Lincoln's adult same-sex relationships beginning at age 22 with Billy Greene in New Salem, Illinois in 1831 and followed by one with Joshua Speed in Springfield beginning in 1837. He shared a bed with Speed for over four years. During Lincoln's presidency, he had intimate relations with Col. Elmer Ellsworth, "a flashy young drillmaster" who died in the early days of the war and later Capt. David Derickson who, in the words of his regiment's history published three decades later, "in Mrs. Lincoln's absence, he frequently spent the night at his cottage, sleeping in the same bed with him."

By contrast to these, Tripp studied Lincoln's special relations with three women including Mrs. Lincoln, all of which were "problematic or distant." Lincoln's untimely death in 1865, like Hamilton at the hand of an assassin, compelled his great admirer, the gay Walt Whitman, to pen his memorable poem "Oh Captain, My Captain." Beyond their common fates, the similarities in the exercise of the gay sensibility between Hamilton and Lincoln are astonishing. Although today's Republicans like to claim them both for their pantheon of heroes, their policies had far more in common with the great Democratic presidents of the 20th century to the present beginning with Franklin D. Roosevelt (whose conscience and sense of doing the right thing was aided immensely by his lesbian wife Eleanor) and his New Deal empowerment of working people and the war against one of the worst, most brutal tyrants in world history, Adolf Hitler.

Lincoln did not shy away from prosecuting a war against a Confederacy that was a proxy for the British who relied on their textile industry for cotton from the southern U.S. states and cynically perpetuated the institutions of slavery and exploitation against disadvantaged people worldwide.

Lincoln freed the slaves, realizing the dream of Hamilton and other Abolitionists, and set in place a set of policies that encouraged a half-century of unprecedented progress that absorbed and provided an unprecedented opportunity for millions of immigrants. These policies included the railroad act, the land grant college act, the greenback currency act, and the Homestead Act.

What "great poets" both Hamilton and Lincoln were! Their lives, their careers, and their passions manifested full measures of their gay sensibility their unique sensual perspective, and their constructive non-conformity. There is little doubt why evidence shows the seminal role of same-sex oriented persons in the development of the U.S., from her spiritual forebears in the Old Testament David to Socrates and the Greek republican model to the pillars of the Renaissance and the emergence of the modern scientific method, to Alexander Hamilton, Walt Whitman, Abraham Lincoln, and Eleanor Roosevelt.

While the Stonewall riots of June 1969 are considered the storied launch of the modern gay movement, they were but one inflection point in the gradual progress of self-esteem and empowerment of same-sex oriented persons in the U.S., progress which accelerated fiercely in the context of the pro-civil rights and anti-Vietnam War ferment of the late 1960s. That progress was integrally tied to notions of human dignity and moral fortitude applied to the struggle for justice and peace for all persons. Regrettably, it was not long after that Stonewall moment that for the gay movement a descent in the early 1970s toward inward-directed hedonistic excess overtook it, and the demand for rights became little more than a demand to perpetuate such excesses without interference.

It makes total sense that from a broad cosmological perspective, that which manifests the fundamental dissymmetry of the unfolding universe would be at the forefront of its progressive change and evolution. In human development on this planet, cosmic dissymmetry is evidenced by a roughly seven-percent deviation from the norm which accounts for such anomalies as left-handedness and primary same-sex orientation in persons. While left-handedness is a physical phenomenon, same-sex orientation is a more-or-less mental one that reveals a predisposition to value reality and sensation from a different vantage point, so to speak. It is not the same-sex orientation that creates this predisposition as is often thought but the other way around. That accounts for why most homosexual persons experience themselves as "different" in early childhood, long before sexual arousal is a factor in their lives, *per se*.

From this standpoint, it is clear that persons manifesting this alternative predisposition embody, as a general rule, the highest potential to be vanguards in the universe's impulse for positive self-development. They bring an alternative sensibility, an alternative perspective, and a natural constructive nonconformity to everything they experience and impact. It is just those features that constantly press humanity to break out from its status quo at any given moment to progress to greater enlightenment, self-consciousness, and the extension of progress to the entire species. Such progress is in the direction of, in human social terms, universal rights and democratic values, and therefore, at any stage, it presses against the normative social organization based on social Darwinism or "might makes right" paradigms. Thus, since the first emergence of human society, we have the struggle of the "poet," the manifestation of dissymmetry and progress, against the tyrant, the "king of the hill" at any given moment, ruling with an iron fist as the dominant male.

In the last century, the notion of "revolution" has had a bad connotation because it has been associated with developments in Russia and China, for example. But those did not produce progressive change, despite claims to the contrary, and were merely the succession of one form of tyranny over another. The last major example of a real revolution advancing humanity was that which resulted in the founding of the United States of America. It was egalitarian advancing democracy rooted in core concepts of the inalienable rights of all persons. Since the founding of the republic and its Constitution, it has progressed toward the fuller realization of those core values by eliminating slavery, granting suffrage to women, outlawing child labor, empowering workers, and spreading such values abroad.

Through all this, tyrants that have resisted these constructive developments have fought against them bitterly. Is there any doubt why they, and the social systems that prop them up, train their young to bully and beat up young poets on the nation's playgrounds and to bash, marginalize and drive them to suicide whenever they can? By the late 1960s, the tyrant paradigm was on the ropes as never before in history. Its slavery was gone, its male-exclusive right to vote was gone, its structural institutions of domination through racism, sexism and, anti-labor thuggery were crumbling like never before. Progress against it had led right into their homes, turning their own chattel, their wives and children, against them. Gay liberation was poised to be a death blow freeing countless of the tyrants' own children to fully actualize their constructive nonconformist revolutionary potential through the process of coming out boldly against any arbitrary social constraints set up to deter them. The fullest liberation of all persons on the planet, to be led by this vanguard, was closer to realization than ever.

A BELOVED COMMUNITY

"Stand up straight, because it's only if you're
bent over that oppressors can hold you down."
—Rev. Martin Luther King

WITH EVERY ADVANCE "GREAT POETS" INSPIRED downtrodden and oppressed people. Those great words of fortitude by Dr. King, as he echoed them at a rally of Memphis sanitation workers just before his assassination in 1968 were at the heart of all struggles for freedom and equality, a struggle that does not end until that imperialist, might-makes-right patriarchal, white male chauvinist tyrant paradigm is finally vanquished once and for all.

In 1968, those of us who knew ourselves to be gay stood with Dr. King in the framework of centuries of "great poet" struggles, taking his words to heart on behalf not only of all peoples but on behalf of ourselves as homosexuals as well. This is what sparked the rise of the modern gay liberation movement. With pioneers like Frank
, Lilli Vincenz, and others igniting the flame in the mid-1960s, following the assassinations of Dr. King and Bobby Kennedy in 1968, it became no longer possible for millions of us who were secretly gay to do anything but stand up straight, in response to Dr. King's admonitions, ourselves.

We claimed the moral integrity and personal liberation associated with Dr. King's call by "coming out proud and fighting" and standing tall by claiming our gayness not only for ourselves but as a beacon of hope to all others, gays, women, minorities, and children laboring under the burden of white male domination and oppression. We would no longer allow society to force us to compromise our integrity and dignity. Living in the closet was living a lie, a structural internalization of the duplicity of spirit and character that led to deceit and self-destruction. Once we came out in that context nothing mattered more than claiming the personal integrity we felt from such a defiant act despite the hostility encountered not only in the wider society but in countless individual households. On all levels, the tyrant paradigm lurched in anger and horror. Combined with the mobilized aspirations of women, minorities, and youth, aroused for civil rights and against the war, the rise of gay liberation from among society's "great poets" its most creative artists, educators, scientists, and humanitarians shook the foundations of that paradigm's very existence.

There is no doubt that the phenomenon we have come to call homosexuality is a derivative of a natural impulse among a certain consistent percentage of the population of all human cultures over time to manifest a heightened empathy toward persons of their sex. In the natural order of things, this is for the essential purpose of bucking the prevailing trend toward fixed social roles for the sexes that subordinate them to male-dominated procreative roles and functions, which include the preparation of males for war and conflict, and females for slavish obedience to men and the perpetuation of the social paradigm through child-rearing. As a natural function of creation, what we call homosexuality inclines a proportion of the dominant population away from total, slavish adherence to this paradigm, and the direction of its progress through enlightenment, empowerment of individual creative potential, universal beauty, and social and governmental institutions that affirm and protect all persons.

This is done through a form of same-sex loving that is not a subordinated function of the dominant social paradigm, but which defies and baffles it, tending to nurture and inspire a wider population to break from brutish, male-dominated behaviors toward to acknowledge and inspire what Lincoln called "the higher angels of our nature." In this, those of us called homosexuals are called to "love that to which we are inclined" and to affirm in the Biblical sense "By the grace of God, I am what I am" by loving the objects of our natural affection, not by exploiting, denigrating, or diminishing them.

In her book, *How the Homosexuals Saved Civilization* (2004), Cathy Crimmins writes, "Looking back, I can see how America fought hard to ignore the gay undertow of our culture from the fifties well into the eighties. There were so many unanswered questions. Why was Paul Lynde the funniest guy on Hollywood Squares? We were Liberace's clothes and jewels the most fabulous? Why were Johnny Mathis ballads the favorite make-out music for heterosexual couples in the sixties? Why were many of the greatest playwrights of the last half of the twentieth century – Tennessee Williams, Lanford Wilson, Terrence McNally, Edward Albee – all gay men writing for straight audiences? Why are Cole Porter's love songs the cleverest and most poignant?"

She names many more creative and accomplished persons in her volume (limited to gay men), from James Beard to Peter Tchaikovsky, Elton John, Noel Coward, W. H. Auden, Tab Hunter, Truman Capote, Nathan Lane, Carson Kressley, David Sedaris, Malcolm Forbes, Harvey Fierstein, Jerome Robbins, Barney Frank, Augusten Burroughs, Craig Clairborne, Leonard Bernstein, Stephen Sondheim, Montgomery Clift, Arthur Laurents, Tony Kushner, Rufus Wainwright, Gore Vidal, Thornton Wilder, Jerry Herman, William Inge, John Waters, Freddie Mercury, George

Michael, Boy George, Clay Aiken, the Village People, David Bowie, James Dean, Ray Davies, Andy Warhol, Pete Townsend, Little Richard, Dick Sargent, Rip Taylor, Charles Nelson Reilly, Rock Hudson, Cary Grant, James Dean, Dirk Bogarde, Anthony Perkins, John Gielgud, George Cukor, Raymond Burr, Richard Chamberlain, Rudolph Valentino, Charles Laughton, Tyrone Power, Sal Mineo, Todd Haynes, Ian McKellen, James Whale, Franco Zeffirelli, Michael York, Isaac Mizrahi, Liberace and more.

While Crimmins acknowledges a gay sensibility factor linking gayness and creativity, I differ on the core matter of causality. Are they creative because they're gay as she suggests, or are they gay because they were born with what I've described as an inherent gay sensibility involving a different sensual perspective and a necessarily constructive non-conformity that are indispensable components of social progress?

THE "OUT AND PROUD" TRUTH

THE BIGGEST PLUS FROM THE LATE 1960s rise of the gay liberation movement was the incredible benefit to homosexuals that being "out and proud" provided. It allowed gay people for the first time to enjoy a level of personal integrity within the larger society that living a lie had denied them for eons. A second key development was the ability to talk, depict and debate same-sex relations openly in literature, media, films, classrooms, and open forums in every conceivable manner, including more recently via the Internet, such that the great silence on the subject throughout most of history was broken at last. This included the rise of gay-themed newspapers in major cities across the U.S., including the *Gay Sunshine* in the San Francisco Bay Area, where I wrote its first editorial and became a prolific writer on gay liberation themes in other local area counterculture print media including the *Berkeley Barb, Berkeley Tribe,* the *San Francisco Kalendar,* and my own *The Effeminist* between 1970 and 1973.

At the same time, a ton of research on gay history was unleashed, resulting in large volumes including Colin Spencer's *Homosexuality in History* (1995), K. J. Dover's *Greek Homosexuality* (1978), Daniel H. Garrison's *Sexual Culture in Ancient Greece* (2000), Louis Compton's *Homosexuality and Civilization* (2003), Francis Mark Mondimore's *A Natural History of Homosexuality* (1996), Vittorio Linardi's *Men in Love: Homosexualities from Ganymede to Batman* (2002), Paul Russell's *The Gay 100* (1995), Thomas Hubbard's *Homosexuality in Greece and Rome* (2003), John Boswell's *Christianity, Social Tolerance and Homosexuality* (1980), Jonathan Katz' *Gay American History* (1992), Robert Aldrich's *Gay Life and Culture: A World History* (2006), Martin Duberman, Martha Vicinis and George Chauney, Jr.'s *Hidden from History: Reclaiming the Gay and Lesbian Past* (1989), Kenneth Stern's *Queers in History* (2009) and more.

All this had not been available before except to the serious scholar. All were written from a value-neutral standpoint, with simply same-sex sexual relations as their common parameters.

Still, they include continuity of important thinkers on gay origins and purpose from Walt Whitman (1819-1892) into the 1970s works of Tennessee Williams (1911-1983) and

Christopher Isherwood (1904-1986). It flowed from Karl Heinrich Ulrichs (1825-1895) to Mangus Hirschfeld (1868-1935), to Edward Carpenter (1844-1929), to E. M. Forster (1879-1970), to Isherwood and Williams.

This was matched on the lesbian side by women's rights and suffrage pioneers including Mary Wollstonecraft (1759-1797), Susan B. Anthony (1820-1906), and Gertrude Stein (1874-1946).

It was Ulrichs who first attempted to integrate gays into a positive wider notion of universal reality as I have sought to do in these installments, more explicitly than Walt Whitman's idea of "great poets." In 1864, under a pseudonym, Ulrichs wrote a series of five booklets called *Researches Into the Riddle of Love Between Men*. In it he expounded a theory of the origins and nature of same-sex erotic attraction, which he attributed to the notion of a female soul trapped in a male body, making for a third sex. He coined the term "urning" or "urania" derived from a reference in Plato's *Symposium* to love between men as "the beautiful love, the heavenly love, the love belonging to the heavenly muse Urania." In 1865 Ulrichs founded the first gay organization ever known, the Uranian Union and despite his arrest in 1867, he persisted as a self-proclaimed "uranian" to fight for the repeal of anti-sodomy laws.

As pioneering gay activist Edward Carpenter wrote in 1908, Karl Heinrich Ulrichs posited a notion of gay identity apart from sexual orientation, *per se*, and remains to this day one of the very few equal rights advocates to do this. In Carpenter's *The Intermediate Sex* (1908), he summarized

Ulrichs' theory about the male "uranian" as follows (as taken from Paul Russell's work):

> He's a man who, while possessing
> thoroughly masculine powers of mind and
> body, combines with them the tenderer and
> more emotional soul-nature of the woman
> – and sometimes to a remarkable degree…
> Emotionally they are extremely complex,
> tender, sensitive, pitiful and loving, 'full of
> storm and stress, of ferment and fluctuation' of
> the heart: the logical faculty may or may not,
> in their case, be well-developed, but intuition is
> always strong; like women, they read characters
> at a glance, and know, without knowing how,
> what is passing in the minds of others; for
> nursing and waiting on the needs of others
> they have often a peculiar gift; at the bottom
> lies the artist-nature, with the artist's sensibility
> and perception. Such a one is often a dreamer,
> of brooding, reserved habits, often a musician,
> or a man of culture courted in society, which
> nevertheless does not understand him.

For the female "uranian," he provides the following:

> The inner nature is to a great extent
> masculine; a temperament active, brave
> and originative, somewhat decisive, not too
> emotional; fond of outdoor life, of games and

sports, of science, politics or even business;
good at organization, and well-pleased with
positions of responsibility, sometimes making
an excellent and generous leader. Such a
woman, it is easily seen, from her social
combination of qualities, is often fitted for
remarkable work, in professional life, or as
manageress of institutions, or even as a ruler
of a country…Many a Santa Clara, or abbess-
founder of religious houses, has probably
been a woman of this type; and in all times
such women – not being bound to men by
the ordinary ties – have been able to work the
more freely for the interests of their sex, a cause
to which their temperament impels them to
devote themselves *con amore*.

This represents the otherwise-almost-non-existent attempt to identify "uranians" in terms of personality type above and preceding sexual orientation, and as such to develop a notion of a gay, or "uranian," identity beyond the domain of sexuality.

It was Carpenter who did the most to advance constructive theories about a universal purpose behind same-sex attraction. In his tract *The Intermediate Sex*, he coined the term "homogenic love" (preferring it to the term homosexual). Carpenter built on the theories of Ulrichs adding that because of their "doubleness," "homogenic lovers" have "special work to do as reconcilers and interpreters of the two sexes to each other." He added that "homogenic love" is a "spiritualized and altruistic comrade attachment" derived from Plato and Whitman's notion of "fervid relationships." He saw same-sex erotic attraction and comradeship as an integral stage in human evolution, an "indication of some important change actually in progress," adding that "certain new types of humankind may be emerging, which will have an important part to play in the societies of the future, even though for the moment their appearance is attended by a good deal of confusion and misapprehension." It was while visiting Carpenter that the already-famous author E.M. Forster wrote that he experienced his own gay awakening derived from something as simple as Carpenter's young partner George Merrill, affectionately patting him on his rear. That resulted in Forster's great novel of gay love *Maurice*, based on Carpenter's and Merrill's relationship which though written in 1914, could not be published (or subsequently made into a motion picture) for general circulation until after Stonewall in 1971.

In the early days of the post-Stonewall movement, I suggested a similar approach to gay identity in the editorial I wrote for the first-ever edition of the *Gay Sunshine* newspaper in 1970. Seeing the gay liberation struggle as an extension of the torrid 1960s civil rights, feminist, and anti-war movements up to that point, I wrote that the new *Gay Sunshine* should be "a newspaper that will represent those who understand themselves as oppressed – politically oppressed by an oppressor that not only is down on homosexuality but equally down on all things that are not white, straight, middle class, pro-establishment…It should harken to a greater cause – the cause of human liberation, of which homosexual liberation is just one aspect – and on that level make its stand." Thus, the proposition was that gay identity is rooted not primarily in sexual orientation, but in common political oppression with others and is thus susceptible to "harken to a higher cause – the cause of human liberation." My San Francisco Bay Area circle and I continued with this approach to gay identity, going on to produce *The Effeminist* newspaper, among other things, seeking to assert gay identity as subsumed in the feminist struggle.

I have come now to refine a concept of gay identity that differs from the Ulrichs-Carpenter "uranian" notion primarily by utilizing the more general concepts, based on the unprecedented idea of a natural and important universal role for gays, or "uranians," whose gay sensibility, an alternative perspective, and constructive non-conformity precede sexual orientation. Unlike Carpenter's British aristocratic perspective, mine draws from the more red-blooded American revolutionary identity inherent in Walt Whitman's "great poet" notion in his *Leaves of Grass*, especially in terms of a disposition for "horrifying despots." We are the people who as nature's essential seven percent, are not bound by a conventional sensibility, who bring a different gay sensibility, and an alternative perspective on reality, necessarily resulting in a penchant for a constructive non-conformity that compels human progress. For that tiny portion of our seven percent that finds itself in the right circumstances, we experience our identity in terms of same-sex attraction.

My argument here is to establish that what primarily defines what society calls us as "homosexuals" lies beyond, or before, the domain or erotic same-sex attraction and behaviors *per se*, and is found in ubiquitous evidence in the chronicles of Western civilization as a unique gay sensibility an alternate perspective and a constructive non-conformity. It is in the areas of creative contributions to all the arts and sciences, including the art of politics, that this unique identity's stamp is seen most clearly. It is also my argument, in this context, that homosexuality is not an aberration or chance of nature, but that it is built into the very fabric of the unfolding of the universe. It is a dissymmetry whose role is to shatter inertia derived from the simple, dominant binary male-female-reproduction-survival nature of things in favor of not merely the survival, but the progress and advance of the species. In other words, homosexual passion is directed toward a different kind of procreation, one which advances the pursuit of beauty, justice, knowledge, and truth, which are different facets of the same thing.

The "poetic principle" at the core of this special role is reflected in Plato's assertion, "Poetry is nearer to vital truth than history." Insofar as it is the inherent role of homosexuals to shatter the cultural status quo wherever their influence can be felt, they become easy targets of angry, brutal repression, and isolation, especially when the status quo is a male-dominated cultural model.

That's because to the extent it is the natural inclination of homosexuals to manifest thirst for justice and to affirm the essential humanity of all, they tend to side with the oppressed, including women, orphans, and the downtrodden, those whose exploitation males in male domination cultures feed upon to buoy their social roles.

Therefore, just as homosexuals are defined by their DNA, so to speak, it is also true that heterosexual males defined in terms of domination over women and military enemies, have it built into their biological memories, their DNA, to hate and seek to hurt homosexuals. Ultimately, the only way for homosexuals to be freed from this oppression, therefore, is for their influence to be felt in society, along with women and other oppressed groups, so strongly that the paradigm of male domination is overthrown in the culture once and for all. It is not by receiving equal rights that this is accomplished, although gains on that front may reflect progress toward the ultimate liberation of homosexuals and all persons from the repressive male chauvinist social paradigm. Equal rights and attitudes of tolerance can be reversed swiftly in any situation where male dominion still rules, and the most unfortunate approach homosexuals can take overall is to attempt assimilation and accommodation to that dominant culture by announcing things such as, "We're just like you, except for who we sleep with."

This is why, from the beginning of the modern gay liberation movement in the developments that surrounded the Stonewall Riots of 1969, I and others with me in the San Francisco area fought to forge alliances with avant-garde feminist and civil rights activists to take on "The Man," the culture that was resisting gains so ferociously of minority, labor, women's and gay rights, and was sending its young sons to jungles halfway around the world where over 50,000 of them died for oil. I lost two friends in Vietnam. I came out as a homosexual in part for that reason. Awakening to the consummate evil of militaristic male-dominated culture marked the single most important event in my life. With the veil of secrecy lifted away from homosexuals, removing the crippling duplicity we were forced to internalize, liberated internal integrity in us all and sprung a heretofore never-experienced potential for a full, unrestrained explosion of gay sensibility on society.

My view of gay identity is premised on two affirmations: that there is an underlying order and purpose to the universe (propelled by a self-developing negative-entropic scientific lawfulness that appears in nature; some may credit God for it) and, within that, same-sex erotic attraction plays a positive, meaningful role. Everything in my explorations is derived from these. In my argument, the role of same-sex erotic attraction as a dissymmetric tendency in the universe unfolds in human history in an uneven and bumpy way. Mother Nature is far from precise, especially in perpetuating an embedded, necessary alternative to the norm that is subject, for that reason, to repression and brutality. Thus, an empirical examination of same-sex erotic attraction and behavior runs the gamut from the most abusive to the most loving – from viewing desired persons as "meat," on the one hand, to "beautiful souls," on the other. Homosexuality's marginal status has made it susceptible to abuse, even as its uncorrupted natural impulse weds erotic attraction and the pursuit of beauty, art, science, and "the good."

The history of homosexuality is far from uniform. Many forms are cruel and exploitative. There's the socially-accepted ritual abuse of prepubescent boys by older men in certain tribes of New Guinea, ancient Cretan pederasty abduction rituals, Spartan-like militaristic cults, present-day practices by tribal leaders in Northern Afghanistan, examined in PBS' 2010 *Frontline* documentary, "The Dancing Boys of Afghanistan," where homeless boys are dressed up as girls to dance and be sexually abused by gatherings of powerful men. For thousands of years, rape and abuse by the rich and/or powerful in political, religious, or other institutions have undoubtedly occurred under a cloak of silence. Still, it is not homosexuality that is to blame. It is man's inhumanity to man, and for most of history, women have seldom fared any better, either.

But by contrast are examples of uplifting and progressive forms of same-sex erotic expression, which elevate beauty and the enduring and loving nurture of the subjects of same-sex love. Throughout history, the vast, vast majority of same-sex oriented persons remained invisible largely because they did not do anything to draw attention but also because so many deigned to follow the humane and empathetic model of Plato and Socrates and their followers focusing their same-sex erotic attractions and love toward advancing notions of beauty, art, learning, and institutions of compassion. Thus, they lived the creative and progressive lives that nature had intended for them.

Few homosexual love letters have persevered through all the years, though gay historian Rictor Norton assembled a bunch in his *My Dear Boy: Gay Love Letters Through the Centuries* (1998). But no case has matched the Sonnets of the English language's greatest pen, William Shakespeare. His Sonnets were published without his approval (thus "outing" him) in 1609 only a few years before his death and they resonate with the highest expression of same-sex love.

There is no mistaking that 126 of the 154 total Sonnets were written as love letters to a young man, the mysterious "Mr. W.H" to which they were all dedicated. In 1766, a scholar named Thomas Tyrwhitt theorized that "Mr. W.H." was an Elizabethan boy actor, Willie Hughes. That theory was based in part on the use of a pun in Sonnet 20 referring to "A man in Hew, all Hews in controlling." That sonnet, considered the first by some scholars began "A woman's face with Nature's hand-painted, hast thou, the master-mistress of my passion." In 1889, gay writer Oscar Wilde wrote a short piece of fiction entitled "The Portrait of Mr. W.H." about this object of Shakespeare's passionate affection. The passion expressed in Shakespeare's Sonnets is breathtaking, revealing a depth of emotion that reminds us of all of our most intensely desired subjects of love. Shakespeare wrote of the "desire of perfect'st love being made" in Sonnet 51, and proclaimed, "So are you to my thoughts as food to life, or as sweet-season'd showers are to the ground" (Sonnet 75).

Shakespeare sang of "the beauty of your eyes and in fresh numbers number all our graces" (Sonnet 17), and in the famous Sonnet 116, he proclaimed the eternal nature of such passionate love:

> ...Love is not love
> Which alters when it alteration finds,
> Or bends with the remover to remove.
> O no! It is an ever-fixed mark
> That looks on tempests and is never shaken;
> It is the star to every wand'ring bark,

Whose worth's unknown, although his height be
 taken.
Love's not Time's fool, though rosy lips and cheeks
Within his bending sickle's compass come;
Love alters not with his brief hours and weeks,
But bears it down even to the edge of doom.

The physical beauty of the present is extended to the eternal beauty of the soul forever, the greatest ever expression of same-sex passion.

While homosexuals had no way to define themselves other than by their sexual orientation, there were efforts in the early days of the modern era. While homosexual was a term imposed by straight society, from within fledgling gay communities efforts at defining what was called a "uranian" sensibility evolved up until World War I. But then that terrible global massacre wiped out the credibility of anything from the softer age of Art Nouveau, optimism and romanticism before it. While managing the ebbs and flows of greater and lesser periods of repression and hate, through the emergence of radio and film gays began to make enormous achievements in the creative arts and other fields while remaining closeted to all but their most intimate circles of friends. Means for social outcasts to connect privately by telephone to meet one another, and assemble in designated secret locations led to the formation of tiny urban "communities" of self-identified homosexuals during the 20th century.

The socially-mandated duplicity that gays were compelled to internalize as they were more visible to the general public via their creative contributions and the emerging mass media, caused them to psychologically bifurcate their creative work from their personal sexual desires. The two, like the double lives they were forced to live, were made to seem unrelated to each other.

Following World War II in the U.S., one of the most remarkable windows of the generosity of spirit involving an entire nation unfolded. Having defeated tyrants to the east and the west, America came out of the war with new confidence and faith in its institutions of justice and mercy. Rather than retribution, it greeted the post-war period by founding the United Nations and launching the reconstruction of Japan and Europe. In 1947, Eleanor Roosevelt led the development of a remarkably progressive and visionary U.N. International Declaration of the Rights of Man. This context, also shaped by the amazing works of Tennessee Williams, led to the advancement of civil rights. It was in this environment that urban homosexuals began looking at themselves in a new way, as not misfits, ingrates, or sinners, but as human beings. By the mid-1960s, a nascent homosexual rights movement became visible.

2

Arrival of an Amoral Sensibility

Burroughs: 'Do what thou wilt' is the whole of the Law.

Williams: Regarding drugs, you mean.

Burroughs: Regarding anything... 'Nothing is true, everything is permitted.' In other words, everything is permitted because nothing is true. If you see everything as illusion, then everything is permitted...

Williams: Provided you want to do the right thing, yes.

Burroughs: Ah, but if you really want to do it, then it's the right thing. That's the point.

Williams: Isn't that an amoralist point of view?

Burroughs: Completely...completely.

Williams: I don't believe you are an amoralist.

Burroughs: Oh yes.

Williams: You do believe it?

Burroughs: Well, I do what I can...

Williams: I don't think it's true.

Burroughs: We were both brought up in the Bible belt; but it's obvious that what you want to do is, of course, eventually what you will do, anyway. Sooner or later.

NOTHING SIGNALED THE DEPARTURE OF THIS amoral sensibility from the earlier gay sensibility than that conversation between Tennessee Williams and the gay radical Beat poet, William Burroughs, published on the pages of the *Village Voice* in May 1977 just as the excesses of impersonal gay sex were well on their way to fueling the outbreak of AIDS. Doing the "right thing" versus "everything is permitted." That sharp contrast defined the separation between the true homosexual sentiment from the horror it became for too many during that awful era.

In an effort to figure out what really happened to homosexuals in America following the magnificent explosion of open self-affirmation that attended the early days of the Stonewall Era, the 1977 Williams-Burroughs exchange functions as a sort of Rosetta Stone. It is the key to unlocking and sorting out how the gay liberation movement went from the highest of the high positive social force to the pit of an AIDS Dark Age, to the lowest of the low, within the course of barely a decade. The implications for today and the movement going forward are also profound. Someone as perceptive and street-savvy as Tennessee Williams was truly surprised by William S. Burroughs' revelation in that exchange, as late in the gay liberation process as 1977, was indicative of the confused state of the movement, and few people even to this day are aware of this distinction, much less of its significance.

With the outburst of post-Stonewall gay liberation in 1969 came an unprecedented opportunity for homosexuals to massively increase and intensify the unique contributions to a just and compassionate wider society that it is innate to our disposition to provide. Homosexuals' creativity, suddenly bolstered by a new level of self-affirmation and esteem, was poised for unleashing on the world its greatest gifts. Williams represented that creativity. An active, happy, and practicing homosexual since the days he plucked chickens in California and worked as a doorman in New York prior to his 1944 breakthrough as a playwright, Williams lived a lively and adventurous gay life. No matter how much he caroused, he did not compromise on his commitment to his creative work. He never abandoned, even in his toughest patches, his routine of hard work writing for lengthy unbroken periods every single morning. He often said his creative work was his life, and was amazingly prolific. He did not define himself by his homosexuality, but by his work.

The counter-cultural ethos that swept over the post-Stonewall gay movement was entirely otherwise. It quickly became grounded entirely in the pursuit of unrestrained gay sex, urged people to "turn on, tune in and drop out" of their creative pursuits, and progressed rapidly to an astounding level of promiscuity and excess. Efforts by myself and others in my "Effeminist" gay liberation current of the early 1970s, including my literary slug fests with Burroughs' pal Allen Ginsberg on the pages of the *Berkeley Barb*, were overwhelmed.

By 1977, at the time of the Williams-Burroughs dialogue, there was only one voice in the wilderness cautioning that there were emerging, dire consequences to the urban gay scenes' descent into a wanton, unbridled, obsessive drug-induced unending orgy of impersonal and extreme sex. The AIDS virus was already spreading among gay men in these environments with an average 5.5-year incubation period to surface with so-called "gay cancer" symptoms in the summer of 1981.

Larry Kramer, who in 1969 wrote the Oscar-nominated screenplay for the film version of D.H. Lawrence's *Women in Love*, was writing his biting novel, prophecy, and critique of what the gay movement had devolved into entitled *Faggots*. The book was reviled by the forgettable leaders of the gay movement including its political leaders, none of whom said a word of caution about what the prevailing gay lifestyle had become. *Faggots* was written as an unyielding challenge to urban gay men to take a hard, critical, self-reflective look at what they had descended into, written in the form of a brutally-explicit novel about the behavior of such men in the Manhattan of that day. Tragically, its accounts were generally not excessive compared to the actual reality and it was incredibly prescient. Among other things, its characters say things like "Faggots don't want to know about success. It reminds them of what they're evading." Its sub-stories of young teenagers coming from rural areas to find themselves, to seek creative success and romance, being dragged into the middle of intense sequences of unrelenting drugged sexual activity with no regard for consequences or human emotions is painful to read, even had the resultant AIDS epidemic that killed most of them not resulted. But even Kramer couldn't see that coming home to roost only three years later.

How Did It All Start?

With the floodgates open at last in the wake of the Stonewall riots, tons of material began being compiled and disseminated on all things homosexual for as far as history would go. It was as if a light switch was suddenly flipped to on. Of the many, many things that issued forth, the most prominent, not surprisingly, was evidence of the institutional repression, hatred, and cruelty perpetrated against anyone who was either caught in a homosexual embrace or who even looked like a sissy or fairy. Throughout history, it was the sissies who were the first to be deployed into quasi-suicidal missions in military campaigns because they were seen as the most expendable and devalued. The death penalty for sodomy was common, notwithstanding specific exceptions, such as the ancient Greeks and Romans.

Prior to 1969, the public's awareness of homosexuality in culture had been generally limited to some vague awareness of those degenerate ancient Greeks, the Biblical condemnations, and the cruel fate imposed on Oscar Wilde for being convicted of "the love that dare not speak its name" with his erstwhile lover Alfred Douglas ("Bosie") in 1895. All references to homosexuality by great gay poets and playwrights like Shakespeare and Walt Whitman were interpreted as something else and Thomas Mann's *Death in Venice* 1912 novella was understood as the pursuit of ideal beauty and not in terms of a same-sex orientation.

Great homosexual literary giants like Tennessee Williams, Christopher Isherwood and E. M. Forster faced the same need to mask the true meaning of many of their works, although in 1947 Williams slipped a homosexual reference into *A Streetcar Named Desire* concerning Blanche's recollection of her young husband, a reference that was edited out of the famous film version.

Isherwood also sidestepped the hugely homosexual contexts of his *Goodbye to Berlin* and *I Am a Camera* works that later morphed into the stage and film productions of *Cabaret*. Forster wrote the gay-themed Maurice in 1913 but couldn't have it published until after his death in post-Stonewall 1971. It also became a beautiful movie after that.

Only after 1969 did both Williams and Isherwood unveil their own homosexuality and the veiled homosexual themes in much of their best work. Williams, who came out in an interview with David Frost in January 1970 with his famous quote "I've covered the waterfront," wrote his first overtly homosexual-themed play *Small Craft Warnings* in 1972. At the same time, he began his memoirs that brought out the central role homosexuality played in his life. By 1976, Isherwood followed suit with an autobiographical work *Christopher and His Kind* that put the thoroughgoing homosexual content into his *Berlin Stories*. Eventually, both Williams and Isherwood, who were friends, published their tell-all extensive diaries and notebooks with Isherwood's from the 1960s period coming out only last fall. Williams did not hold back describing his cavorting among sailors on the palisades above Santa Monica during the nightly blackouts in 1943.

Before 1969, the portrayal of "fairies" in the movies were harshly prohibited by the Hays Code adopted in 1934 to censor American films for morality and in effect until 1968. While gays were a major force in all the arts throughout that era, they were completely hidden from public view. There were tragic outcomes, such as the suicide of a young, handsome leading man Ross Alexander in 1937. Starring in 1935 with Errol Flynn and Olivia de Havilland in the swashbucking *Captain Blood*, Alexander's homosexuality was well known in inner Hollywood circles but, as with so many gays, he married a woman. His double life drove his wife into depression resulting in her suicide a year before Alexander took his own life. Double lives under the threat of exposure and ruin characterized the lives of many in the pre-Stonewall era. The only portrayals that made the screen were *The Children's Hour* and *Victim* in 1961 when the first cautious steps to open the subject up were taken. Both films however, presented a very troubled and painful view of homosexuality, leading to ruin, blackmail, and suicide. *Victim*, a British film starring Dirk Bogarde, was intended as a compassionate argument for ending the laws against sodomy.

Shining the light on the recorded history of homosexuality also showed that from the beginning same-sex relations were often based on inequalities in age and station with few cases of long-term sustainability. The earliest case was an abduction by the greatest of the Greek gods, Zeus, of the prettiest boy among mortals, Ganymede. At least Zeus arranged a good job for Ganymede as the cupbearer of the gods and later honored him by positioning him in the heavens as the constellation Aquarius. The myth reflected the most common form of homosexual relations documented in ancient Greek and Roman cultures covering over 1,000 years, that involving older men and younger boys who reached their "full height," as in their upper teens (citing K.D. Dover, *Greek Homosexuality*, 1978). According to the historical record, almost all identified homosexual relations, at least up until the modern era, involved inequalities of age and station in society, the paradigm being the Greek-Roman model of an older man of wealth seeking liaison with a younger lad, commonly in search of the older's money, gifts, and pathways to success in later life. Records of such trysts ranged from more acceptable ones among free men to less savory encounters involving slaves and prostitutes.

While such disparities are disquieting to modern sensibilities, if not illegal, in the ebbs and flows of history in the West a higher regard for the potentially virtuous nature of such relations was held in times that roughly correlated to eras of great cultural, scientific, and political advance, such as in the fourth and fifth centuries B.C. in Greece and the height of the Italian Renaissance in the 15th and early 16th centuries A.D. In both those periods, the writings of Plato, *The Symposium* and *Phaedrus* were models for discourses on the role of ethics and morality in those relations. Arguments ranged from limiting expectations to purely non-abusive pleasure-seeking to considering the younger participant's well being psychologically and over the long haul to Plato's and Socrates' case for restraining from sex, but to use the erotic impulse as a driver to introduce higher notions of love, friendship and a love for beauty, and truth into the relationship.

In that order, the three Greek words for love, "eros" as sexual desire, "philia" as friendship and "agape" as divine or universal love, are summoned as applied to the three stages of the Plato/Socrates option, and they all are deployed in that fashion as well in the myth of Ganymede.

First concerning that myth, it should be noted that, insofar as it was Zeus, the highest of the gods, who initiated the relationship, it signals that in the ultimate order of things there is a proper and sanctified role for same-sex passion. While most of Zeus' appetite was for women, his Ganymede caper showed that a role for homosexuality in the eyes and desires of the top god was OK.

Second, the disparity in ages and rank not only reflected the prevailing cultural norm (Dover's researches indicate in that era there was no record of any other kind of homosexual relations, at least that were sanctioned or reported) but was symbolic of the kind of inequality that is, on a personal level, endemic to most relationships: one party usually having some, even nuanced, role difference from the other (one more active than passive, for example) that belies the exact notion of equality as a political and legal term. As terms best to describe interpersonal relations, "complementarity" and "reciprocity" are better choices. In the disparity of roles, the issue lies in what each party brings to the other and whether it is net zero sum in nature, a reciprocity that fulfills the expectations, goals and gratifications of both. Of course, all unequal interactions bear an acute potential for abuse and cruelty, such as especially when one lacks the maturity for discerning powers of free choice, which is why the matter of the true meaning of love, versus abuse and exploitation, is always so important.

In the Ganymede myth, Zeus, synonymous among the Greeks with our notion of God as the creative force of the universe, embraces Ganymede, the archetypal representation of same-sex passion, brings him to a heavenly purpose as servant to the oversight of human affairs (the gods on Olympus). Then finally he elevates and sanctifies him, lifting him to the status among the twelve gears of the universe in the sky as the constellation Aquarius in the Zodiac, by which the entire universe is governed and unfolds, and from whence the very notions of beauty and truth are derived. Ganymede is transported by Zeus through the three powers of love, in its eros, philia and agape manifestations, for purposes of aligning human behavior in accordance with the divine purpose present in the homosexual impulse.

LOVE OF EQUALS

THE PROBLEM IS THIS: WE POST-STONEWALL gays are collectively an entirely new species, being fully open and here for the first time in the history of the species, yet we have yet to define ourselves to ourselves. Indicative of this problem is the inability of any of the post-Stonewall historians, who have worked so diligently to fill in the cavernous silences on matters of same-sex relations over the centuries, to describe same-sex desires and practices in any terms other than the pursuit of pleasure. Even in the rare cases where efforts at sustainable relationships are found in the record, the homosexual act is understood in terms solely of the pleasure derived from it. This is not surprising since the sexual act in the heterosexual context is clearly geared to procreation. There is no such procreative element to a same-sex encounter, so, they argue, it can be explained only by the pleasurable experience it brings. Yet, an alternative interpretation of the meaning of gay sex has been here all along, one that does not deny the procreative role of sex but embraces it fully and gives gay sexual desire a special role in creation.

In mythic-poetic form, it is contained in the ancient Greek myth of Ganymede, and it is spelled out more explicitly by the aged female prophet Diotima in *The Symposium*. Erotic attraction for purposes of reproduction is one of the two greatest driving forces of life. It and the mother's protection of her young account for the perpetuation and survival of the species, and nothing is more important to Mother Nature than this. When the same powerful erotic attraction is found to be directed in the case of some (the ancient Greek Zodiac has it at one, Ganymede/Aquarius, in 12, a plausible proportion) to the same, not opposite sex, then it is also designed to perpetuate the species. But it goes beyond the simple physical acts of reproduction and protection, which do nothing to account for the progress of the species, but only its survival. Erotic attraction (which Diotima says is itself a "spirit") to the same sex provides the passionate ground for the cultivation of beauty and truth in both parties. "When a man, starting from this sensible world and making his way upward by right use of his feeling of love for young men, begins to catch sight of that beauty…This is the right way of approaching or being initiated into the mysteries of love, to begin with examples of beauty in this world, and using them as steps to ascend continually with that absolute beauty as one's aim...from physical beauty to moral beauty, and from moral beauty to the beauty of knowledge, until from knowledge of various kinds one arrives at the supreme knowledge whose sole object is that absolute beauty, and knows at last what absolute beauty is," Diotima says.

The most passionate of erotic attractions and of sexual desire, when drawn from attraction to one of the same sex, is present in creation not simply to devour pleasure, but to be the compelling force that directs both the lover and loved toward a higher and higher appreciations of beauty and knowledge, which leads to universal justice. "There are some [gays] whose creative desire is of the soul, and who long to beget spiritually, not physically, the progeny which it is the nature of the soul to create and bring to birth. If you ask what that progeny is, it is wisdom and virtue in general; of this all poets and such craftsmen as have found out some new thing may be said to be begetters; but far the greatest and fairest branch of wisdom is that which is concerned with the due ordering of states and families, whose name is moderation and justice," Diotima proclaims.

With Stonewall, for the first time since this was written 2,500 years ago, we come onto the scene of history capable of fully embracing and advancing such a potent force of the universe.

Reviewing the long historical record of matters concerning same-sex erotic attraction in the West that's come to light in the years since Stonewall, there are two important overarching summary points to be made. The first is the pervasive way in which homosexual identity shapes every aspect of a gay person's life, expressed through the qualities

I've identified as gay sensibility "alternative perspective" and "constructive non-conformity," whether they are "openly gay" or not.

The second is the historical divergence between expressions of same-sex erotic attraction. Amid the silence and darkness of civilizations since the ancient Greeks with no mass media, no investigations exposing patterns of abuse within the corridors of power and silence, the attraction is expressed through dangerous, marginalized, and only sometimes sanctioned sexual acts. On the other hand, it is expressed in the myth of Ganymede and the writings of Plato, homosexual passions are directed to the care, uplifting, and cultivation of the creative powers of the subjects of such love. On both points, I defer to our great Patron Saint, Tennessee Williams to comment through his writings. On the subject of homosexual identity, he remarks through a soliloquy by his character, Mrs. Venable in the opening section of *Suddenly Last Summer* (1958), speaking about her late homosexual son, Sebastian:

> It still shocks me a little to realize that Sebastian Venable the poet is still unknown outside of a small coterie of friends, including his mother. You see, strictly speaking, his life was his occupation... Sebastian was a poet! That's what I meant when I said his life was his work because the work of a poet is the life of a poet, and vice-versa, the life of a poet is the work of a poet. I mean you can't separate them...

> I mean – well, for instance, a salesman's
> work is one thing and his life is another – or
> can be. The same thing's true of – doctor,
> lawyer, merchant, thief! – But the poet's life
> is his work and his work is his life in a special
> sense.

In this play, Williams still identifies homosexuals with poets just as the gay poet Walt Whitman did in the 1800s and also the seminal influence on Williams, the brilliant but tragic gay poet Hart Crane. Williams thought of himself primarily as a poet, growing up writing poetry and in what he called his "nomadic period," there was an entire time when the only book he carried in his possession contained only Crane's works. When he died accidentally in February 1983, Williams had prepared a speech to deliver to students in New York in which he reiterated that he would want to be remembered as a poet.

The identity of the poet, a.k.a. homosexual in Williams' meaning, is permeated through and through him or her, coloring everything about one's internal soul and sensibility and every creative contribution one makes to the world. While permeated with the soul of the poet defining everything about them, homosexuals focused their lives and passions on elevating the objects of their attraction to higher domains of social sensibility and behavior. The pursuit of the "good" in the Platonic sense was described by Tennessee Williams in a more modern, vernacular sense.

Writing in 1947, he said, "Then what is good? The obsessive interest in human affairs, plus a certain amount of compassion, and moral conviction, that first made the experience of living something that must be translated into pigment or music or bodily movement or poetry or prose or anything that's dynamic and expressive – that's what's good for you if you're at all serious in your aims."

The "good" to Williams, just as with Plato, lies in the cultivation of compassionate, creative potential for the general good, based on an "obsessive interest in human affairs." In the silence of history, a preponderance of homosexuals channeled their passions to such objectives, especially in the context of the patterns of brutal abuses that characterized common society. We see these sisters and brothers in the forging and maintenance of institutions and practices of compassion, morality and purpose.

The Bonds of Moralism

> "The liberation of sexuality from the bonds
> of moralism has left in its wake a crying need
> for principled, intelligent, vigorous explorations
> of how a genuine morality can be introduced
> into our newly minted freedom"
>   – Tony Kushner, introduction to
>   Larry Kramer's *Faggots*

THIS SUCCINCT STATEMENT BY THE GREAT contemporary playwright who brought us *Angels in America* in 1993 sums up precisely my intent through the course of this book (and the "Gay Science" columns from which it is derived). *Morality* is one of the most highly-charged words in our language, one of the most abused and feared. But that a "genuine morality" is important is without question. There is a crying need for it with the emphasis equally on both words and that's why it is conditional upon three other words: principled, intelligent and vigorous. From what I can see, for homosexuals it has never been systematically attempted. My efforts at exploring a "genuine gay morality" have centered on identifying qualities of gay sensibility and creative, constructive nonconformist potential linked to erotic same-sex attraction as a starting point, and examining the implications of that from different perspectives.

The death of renowned atomic physicist Maurice Goldhaber in 2011 helped to bring to light, through lengthy obituaries, his work in the discovery of a fundamental "left-handed" component to the elemental, subatomic structure of physical reality. This discovery about particles known as "neutrinos," which according to the obituary by the *New York Times*' Kenneth Chang, "violate mirror symmetry" of the universe, brought to light something "odd and unexpected" about physical space, contradicting Newton's Law of Motion. A critical experiment by Goldhaber showed that unlike the illustrative case of arrows whose rotation one way is, if reflected in a mirror seen moving in an opposite rotation, neutrinos always rotate in one direction (counterclockwise) and never the other. Already in over my head on this subject, I raise it claiming nothing other than to show there is evidence in physics of what I've contended about a lawful dissymmetry built into the fabric of a universe that, among other things, accounts for homosexuality. Dissymmetry propels the universe's motion away from a static equilibrium to "negentropic" development and manifests itself in the human social sciences in lawfully off beat epiphenomena such as left-handedness, right-brain domination, and homosexuality.

Wrestling with that tension throughout history has been at the core of a homosexual "genuine morality" experienced in ways more acute and painful than for those of the dominant heterosexual culture. It occurred almost exclusively in isolation and dread without solid social guidelines and reinforcements, burdening the homosexual with an overwhelming level of personal responsibility for his or her behaviors.

> "Kings are interested not in the morality but
> the docility of their subjects"
> —St. Augustine, *City of God*

With the industrial revolution, a natural tension developed between the captains of industry and their burgeoning work forces. From the mid-19th century on, industrialists and their monied associates devised strategies to blunt efforts of workers to organize and utilize collective action to achieve economic and social justice. The 1960s bogus quasi-Marxist theory that homosexuals were repressed by capitalists because they undermined the production of stable, obedient households of workers (i.e. Herbert Marcuse, *Eros and Civilization*, 1962) was only partly true.

In Nazi Germany, while homosexuals were tolerated in the ranks of the socially-amorphous Brownshirts to help Hilter overthrow the existing order, they were turned on by the militant Blackshirts during the infamous "Night of the

Long Knives" in the summer of 1934. Subsequently, the Nazis systematically rounded up homosexuals along with Jews and gypsies and sent them to death camps. Urban homosexuals had been supporters of progressive Social Democratic regimes in Germany prior to Hitler's takeover in England and the U.S. In America, Tennessee Williams voted for the Socialist presidential candidate Norman Thomas in 1932.

Meanwhile, when thousands of World War I veterans assembled in Washington, D.C., known as the "Bonus Army," in the Great Depression's dismal summer of 1932 to demand their pensions, Republican President Herbert Hoover called out the U.S. Army against them. Later, after President Franklin D. Roosevelt was elected, many of the same who'd backed the use of the Army against U.S. citizens plotted a military coup against Roosevelt. Often, they were openly pro-Nazi and pro-fascist.

After World War II, these same elements fueled the so-called "Red Scare" and the McCarthyite reign of terror against pro-labor elements in the U.S. government and wider society, accusing them of being communist sympathizers or spies. This came just as redoubled efforts at homosexual rights organizations like the Mattachine Society and Daughters of Bilitis were spearheaded by activists like Harry Hay, a former communist, and backers of Henry A. Wallace's Progressive Party presidential campaign of 1948. In 1953, right wing forces in the newly-formed CIA launched a systematic effort to undermine pro-labor, pro-civil rights currents running strong in the U.S. citizenry at that point. Their covert program was dubbed "MK Ultra," as subsequent Congressional and other investigations revealed in the mid-1970s.

Unable to impose Hitler-style fascism from the top down, MK Ultra and other covert operations were designed to undermine the nation's pro-labor current from within, again, inducing radical individualism and hedonism. From 1952-1972, the project funded and coordinated 149 sub-projects for research of "radiation, electro-shock, various forms of psychology, sociology, anthropology, graphology and paramilitary devices and materials for behavior control, behavior anomaly production and countermeasures." In 1973, CIA Director Richard Helms ordered all files associated with these operations destroyed, but a cache of 20,000 documents had been misfiled and therefore were eluded to destruction. They became the substance of investigations by the Presidential Rockefeller Commission in 1974 and the Congressional Church Committee in 1975 and were made public.

Operating on 44 U.S. college campuses and with 15 research foundations, MK Ultra involved mass experiments with the psychedelic drug LSD and other drugs, aimed at "behavior control," "behavior anomaly production," and "producing predictable human behavioral and psychological changes." Ken Kesey was a key figure who emerged in the early 1960s to play a major role in a cultural sea-change of the American consciousness that involved LSD in a self-centering, hedonistic dumbing down of society. Kesey was recruited to be part of MK Ultra experiments in California and he became a seminal influence, organizing "Be-Ins" involving mass LSD ingestion by youths at beach parties around the San Francisco Bay Area and his famous cross-country bus trip to meet Harvard's LSD guru Timothy

Leary, chronicled in his *Electric Kool Aid Acid Test*. Thus did America's right wing launch the anarchist, radical hedonist 1960s counterculture as a radical flank against the progressive gay movement. I saw it first hand. I was an eyewitness.

3

The Science of Same-Sex Orientation

THE TERM, "HOMOSEXUAL," WAS FIRST COINED in 1869, in Germany. Attentive readers have recognized that some time back, I switched from using the term, "homosexual," and went with "gay." That was intentional, using the former term at first to make it clear, in today's parlance, who I was talking about, and then to lay the basis for a sharp critique of it. Soft-spoken but intense debates raged among radical Enlightenment figures in 1750-1850 in Europe and the young American republic about ameliorating harsh penalties for sodomy. Thomas Jefferson was considered progressive calling for an end to the death penalty at one point, and all laws against it were abolished for a time following the Napoleonic wars in France.

There was no doubt that same-sex affection and bonding played major roles in the revolutions in the U.S. and France, and continued to inflame political passions elsewhere in Europe. The core of the revolutionary spirit against political and social tyrannies was a rejection of the paradigm of male domination over women, children, slaves and culture and the associated militaristic zeal for expanding and controlling territory and resources. Commensurate with this revolutionary zeal, and in the context of a new surge in the value of science and knowledge, rejecting authoritarian church-related mythologies, radical Enlightenment currents orbiting around the collective *Histoire Philosophique* (1770) project led by Denis Diderot (1713-1784), A. G. Raynal (1713-1796) and others in Paris (Jonathan I. Israel, *Democratic Enlightenment*, 2011), began embracing ideas of radical feminism and the validity of same-sex erotic attraction. That was spurred by historian Johann Joachim Winckelmann (1717-1768) and his extensive published catalogs of images of often homo-erotic ancient Greco-Roman art in his *Reflections Concerning the Imitation of the Greeks* (1755) and *History of Ancient Art* (1763).

Winkelmann's enormous influence in the Enlightenment was of keen interest to the great German poet Johann Wolfgang von Goethe (1749-1832), who was likely also gay (Alice A. Kuzniar, ed., *Outing Goethe and His Age*, 1996). Goethe's embrace of erotic same-sex relations was mirrored in the work of the poet Friedrich Schiller (1759-1805), who elevated same-sex passion to the level of Promethean revolution in *Don Carlos* (1787).

In the context of all this, in 1851 a paragraph was added to the Prussian Penal Code, the infamous Paragraph 143, prescribing five years of hard labor for persons convicted of same-sex "unnatural fornication." It was a key inflection point in the push-back by the forces of counter-revolution that began recognizing the correlation between revolution and same-sex passion. Suddenly the counter-revolutionary mandate became to define what was "normal," male-dominating patterns and institutions reinforcing the subjugation of women, families, and properties, and states deriving from that construct. Such a blueprint of male dominion required alienating, through social labels and laws, those who failed or refused to buy into that paradigm.

Thus, by 1869, the socio-political terms of "heterosexual" and "homosexual" were established to counter-revolutionary ends. "Heterosexual" became the code word defining behavior encompassing all that was wrapped up in the male-dominion paradigm. "Homosexual," and all its variants described by Richard von Krafft-Ebing (1840-1902) in his *Psychopathia Sexualis* (1886), became the code for all deviations from that model paradigm. These labels arose for different purposes than explained by conventional wisdom, such as in Charles Upchurch's *Before Wilde: Sex Between Men in Britain's Age of Reform* (2009) or Hanne Blank's *Straight, the Surprisingly Short History of Heterosexuality* (2012). Those explanations fail to grasp the new, late 19th century "science of sexology" in this socio-political context.

The recent degeneration of American right wing political dialogue into an angry Neanderthal assault on women, highlighted by the Virginia legislature's consideration of mandatory intrusive ultrasound procedures with abortions and Rush Limbaugh's utterly contemptible slurs that should get him fired, illustrates that the root of its similarly bigoted anti-gay venom is a violent and raw male supremacist impulse. Some 150 years ago it was this same impulse, having grudgingly given ground to an advance of egalitarian democratic ideals with the abolition of slavery but as yet far from willing to concede any modicum of equality to women, that devised the socio-psychological categories of heterosexual and homosexual. The 1869 demarcation for the first time sought to cordon off a strict definition of an acceptable, male chauvinist-grounded social construct from all other deviations from that norm. It was a counterrevolutionary reaction to the influence of free-thinking women and same-sex eroticism that was fueling ongoing anti-despotic ferment.

In 1962 Gerald Heard, an early member of the Mattachine Society, called us "isophyls," saying he hoped that "isophyls... can see that they are not a freak but a social psychophysical mutation without which our society can't advance." (James T. Sears, *Behind the Mask of the Mattachine*, 2006). Heard's concept is central to my own argument that in nature, we are different for a reason. In his exhaustive, 750-page *Biological Exuberance: Animal Homosexuality and Natural Diversity* (1999), biologist and linguist Bruce Bagemihl documents the massive evidence of same-sex behavior in wildlife. From it he coined the term, "biological exuberance," contrasting the notion post-Darwinian concepts of natural selection evolution, random chaos theory, or biodiversity studies. However, he was the first to admit that the term doesn't explain much, if anything, as animal non-reproductive behaviors remain "paradoxically, inexplicable, since they continue to elude conventional definitions of usefulness. Nothing, in the end, has really been explained."

In *Evolution's Rainbow: Diversity, Gender, and Sexuality in Nature and People* (2004, 2009), evolutionary biologist Joan Roughgarden presents similar material and argues that "the diversity of gender and sexuality make evolutionary sense." She challenges one of Darwin's three claims that in species changes through natural selection, males and females obey universal templates, "the males ardent and the females coy." She suggests a new theory called "social selection" that envisions "animals as exchanging help in return for access to reproductive opportunity," that "animals evolve (social-inclusionary) traits that qualify them for inclusion in groups that control resources for reproduction and safe places to live and raise offspring." These traits are "interpreted as a secondary sex characteristic," and are attributed to what she calls a "genial gene" that counters the commonly-held "selfish gene."

More light on the view expressed here is shed by Jonah Lehrer in "Kin and Kind: A Fight About the Genetics of Altruism" in the March 5, 2012 edition of *The New Yorker* magazine. He notes that Darwin "regarded the problem of altruism – the act of helping someone else, even if it comes at a steep personal cost – as a potentially fatal challenge to his theory of natural selection." Lehrer asks, "Can true altruism even exist? Is generosity a sustainable trait? Or are living things inherently selfish, our kindness nothing but a mask?" He cites the work of entomologist E. O. Wilson, who studied woodpeckers among other things, noting the concept of "group selection, an explanation that most evolutionary biologists now dismiss, because the advantages of generosity are much less tangible than the benefits of selfishness." But

Wilson thinks it is the key to understanding altruism. Citing cases of "cooperating" microbes, plants, and even female lions, "clumps of cooperators thrive and replicate, while selfish groups wither and die." Wilson wrote in 2007, "Selfishness beats altruism within groups. Altruistic groups beat selfish groups." He concludes that "what makes us human is that our history is shaped by both (altruistic and selfish) forces. We're stuck in between."

Altruism as a concept, in the context of normative, fundamentally selfish male dominated society, is akin to preponderant traits of non-normative types, and is indispensable for the success of society. That accounts for us. The thought-through implications of the bio-evolutionary and genetic evidence for what can be called "altruism" as a central, indispensable component for the successful survival and evolution of species are truly astounding and revolutionary, especially as they bear upon questions of the normalcy and necessity of same-sex erotic attraction.

Wilson's work focused on the "advantages of generosity" versus the "benefits of selfishness" in the success of species observed in nature, and found that the former trumps the latter when it comes to the ability of groups to "thrive and replicate." The flawed empiricism that accompanied the late 19th and early 20th century bio-evolutionary and sociological studies succumbed to reductionist categorizations of "heterosexual and homosexual" in the new "sexology" components of their work, perceived to be logical subsets of what rabidly male-chauvinist cultural prejudice superimposed as Darwinian "universal templates" for sexual behavior between males and females. Given those normative templates, same sex erotic behavior was categorized as a deviation from the heterosexual norm, and thereby deviant, either a corruption due to flaws or weaknesses, or a random variant with no real evolutionary consequence.

For some homosexuals, taking on society's negative verdict was translated into a form of individuality and freedom in urban centers where they could cluster and enjoy a modicum of protection and anonymity. There, some took on a collective, special kind of nominal self-esteem. However, it was barely skin-deep, although it accounted for survival and mutual support, and eventually became a launch-pad for the modern gay liberation movement.

Still, this verdict itself was deeply flawed, obfuscating the stunning discovery being presented in this book that the genus of same-sex erotic attraction is not a variant of the heterosexual reproductive impulse or template at all. Instead, it is a manifestation of "species love." Evidence from history has shown since ancient Greece a strong connection between same-sex erotic attraction and social progress. It is a connection, as I have documented extensively, inclined to overthrow arbitrary tyranny in favor of an extension of institutions of justice (including for women, orphans, and slaves), legally-constituted democracy, negotiation over war, and the promotion of invention, science and universal education against tyrannically imposed superstition and fear.

This connection represents in human evolution and progresses the operation of the same kind of altruism that Wilson observed in his natural studies. As with Wilson's studies, that impulse is in constant tension with that of selfishness, and especially with those prevailing in "might makes right" and "survival of the fittest" struggles by the strongest, most always aggressive and deadly males among a species. This tension exists throughout nature and human history. Its pervasiveness and permanence account for why forces of altruism have always fought to establish lasting institutions as bastions of strength and perseverance against perennial onslaughts of "might makes right" tyrannical impulses. That's why Platonists established city-states in Greece, King David solidified a just kingdom, Augustine strengthened the church against the unraveling of a brutal empire and imminent Dark Age, Italian Renaissance leaders replicated the Greek city-state model, Erasmus sought to educate Christian princes, and the enlightened leaders of the Enlightenment saw crafting democratic constitutions as important to overthrowing tyrannies as the revolutions, themselves. That's why Alexander Hamilton and Abraham Lincoln both invoked the notion of "preservation of the union," Hamilton in the Federalist Papers, and Lincoln in the prosecution of the Civil War – to secure institutions of justice against tyranny.

Hamilton and Lincoln both saw the horny hand of greed and tyranny lurking behind the calls for division in their times. Hamilton knew that the colonies could not endure unless united, and the War of 1812 proved him right. Lincoln knew the same fate awaited a divided union, that the Confederacy would soon revert to British colonial subjugation, the dependency of a slave-based cotton trade. The Civil War was both to emancipate the slaves and to preserve the young nation in a century when the main European powers were unbridled in their lust for empire.

The genus of same-sex erotic attraction is not a corruption or variant of a procreative sexual impulse, but is a vital component of nature's effective survival and evolutionary impulse through altruism, empathy and bonding. This important realization not only redefines same-sex attraction outside the reductionist concepts of "sexology," but extends even to more primordial forces in nature, including as evidenced by the "left-handed neutrino" phenomenon discovered by atomic physicist Maurice Goldhaber (discussed earlier as "violating mirror symmetry" of the universe). Not only does this point to an engine of an underlying "negative-entropic" tendency for the universe to self-develop, it is of the same order of reality as the evidence of an indispensable "altruism" in social development of species discovered by entomologist Wilson that defies empiricist interpretations of Darwin's theories. Same-sex erotic attraction plays a critical role in this process – its progenitor being no less than the self-development of the universe, itself – in human social contexts, working to progress society from non-productive male chauvinist-dominated tyranny forms to constitutional, egalitarian democratic ones.

The 18th century mathematician and philosopher Gottfried Wilhelm Leibniz (1646-1710) espoused a concept of the "monad," the notion that everything in the universe is recapitulated in its every singularity, that applies here. Platonists in ancient Greece understood the concept of "species love," defining it in terms of the broad spectrum of "loves" that range from *philia* (brotherly) to *agape* (spiritual) to *eros* (erotic). Although almost no one operating within the matrix defined by a male-dominant species reproduction mode understands this, none of these Platonic-defined "loves" are associated with procreation, either the act of intercourse or the subsequent "motherly love" of child rearing, but instead that they are singled out to define a range for the kind of love that bonds and develops cultures. Same-sex erotic ("*eros*") attraction is a natural variant among these, no matter how much it may appear to emulate the procreative impulse. For any individual "called" to this kind of loving, that loving can be expressed in any one of the three ways, and can also express such loving as "*agape*" or "*philia*" without an "*eros*" component, at all. But they are all related.

In 1912, just over 100 years ago, the sinking of the Titanic on April 15 was perhaps an omen for a century sparked by the June 1914 launch of the Great War, the first of two World Wars, the rise of totalitarian regimes, mass genocides, the AIDS epidemic, a Great Depression and perhaps a second. Another omen was German author Thomas Mann's 1912 novella, *Death in Venice*, about a doomed relationship between a burned out, aging composer and a young teenage lad, a relationship in which no words were exchanged. Smitten by the Polish lad staying in the same vacation hotel in Venice, the composer, Aschenbach, was unable to either hide his interest or speak to the boy. The boy, Tadzio, responded to the interest, but also remained mute. The story ends with the composer's death from cholera on the beach, watching the slightly effeminate object of his attraction wade into the water and pause, left arm extended in a *contrapposto* pose.

Mann's story was based on actual events, on a vacation he took to Venice in the summer of 1911, and the boy was discovered decades later to be a real person, Wladyslaw Moes (1900-1986).

American author Gilbert Adair reconstructed Moes' life history and wrote a short biography, *The Real Tadzio: Thomas Mann's Death in Venice and the Boy Who Inspired It* (2001). "Tadzio," living in Poland, was pushed and pulled his whole life between the two great wars and fascist German and communist Soviet occupations, serving in the Polish military and as a prisoner of war. He grew into and remained "something of a dandy to the end of his life, no mean achievement in Communist Poland," Adair wrote. "Capable of charming the birds off trees," he "prided himself on his grace as a dancer." He married and had children, but otherwise had an uninspired life buffeted by the great social and military convulsions of his age.

There was more than physical beauty that attracted Aschenbach to young Tadzio in the novella. There was something in Tadzio's demeanor, his charm, his way of carrying himself. Also, as Tadzio gazed back at Aschenbach, almost as if he foresaw his future trapped into conformity with a straight male-dominated century of war and fascism, was his silent plea, "Aren't you going to save me?" Aschenbach couldn't. Gay Liberation is supposed to save the Tadzios of our time, to give them the space and the language to fulfill their full potentials to the benefit of all mankind.

It is a critical realization that same-sex erotic attraction is a variant within the role that nature has assigned for its organic survival and evolutionary self-sustenance to the altruistic impulse among persons. A recent scientific discovery is revolutionary, that species survival and evolution are not driven only by self-preservation, reproduction and accidental mutation, but also by an altruistic impulse. Until this discovery, modern Darwinian evolutionary science has dismissed notions of altruism, selfless behavior or love as, effectively, chimeras or extensions of behaviors defined within narrow confinements of "survival of the fittest" and "natural selection" dogma.

Within that, the only explanation for same-sex erotic attraction has been as a corruption or deviation from the reproductive impulse. All modern "sexology" theory over the last 150 years has adopted this core assumption.

As such, this flawed epistemology of "sexology" theory was associated with a current of thought developed in the 19th century as the rise of modern industrialism and imperialism compelled ruling elites to design sociological means to maintain their advantage against much larger bodies of workers and subject peoples and prevent, for example, something like the American revolution from ever happening again. They sought to isolate persons from each other by promoting theories of anarchy and nihilism, reshaping self-perceptions and individual behaviors away from tendencies to bond together and act on the basis of common interests in social development. A seminal influence for this was German philosopher Max Stirner (1806-1856), a founder of nihilism, existentialism, postmodernism, anarchism and post-structuralists like Michel Foucault. Stirner's *The Ego and His Own: The Case of the Individual Against Authority* (1844) shaped similar theories espoused later by the nihilist philosopher Friedrich Nietzsche (1844-1900) and the Italian fascist dictator Benito Mussolini (1883-

1945), demonstrating the cohesion between radical anarchy and fascist dictatorships that represses popular will through totalitarian force.

The psychologist Sigmund Freud (1856-1939), the most influential figure in the "sexology" movement, developed his theories under the umbrella of the same flawed constructs as Stirner and Nietzsche. In his thought, they took the form of a tension between the Id (in terms taken by Nietzsche from Greek mythology, Dionysian) and the Ego (Apollonian), or between raw hedonistic selfish impulse and socially-acceptable identity. But as I established earlier, in terms of Greek mythology, there is a third current, the Promethean, which corresponds to the critical bonding, altruistic influences associated with same-sex attraction that Stirner, Nietzsche, Freud, Mussolini and Foucault denied exists.

Still, our current in fact does exist, and always has, as a substantial reality. In the last century, two powerful manifestations – at least one of a non-erotic variety – can be credited with no less than saving America, defeating tyrannies on two global war fronts and preventing the impact of two world wars and a depression from resulting in tyranny at home. Franklin D. Roosevelt and Eleanor Roosevelt, in tandem the most powerful, unitary influence for good during the entire 20th century, each were beneficiaries of highly influential same-sex bonding experiences. In H. W. Brands' *Traitor to His Class: the Privileged Life and Radical Presidency of Franklin Delano Roosevelt* (2008), writings by Secretary of the Navy Josephus Daniels (1862-1948) state that when Daniels first met Roosevelt in 1912 "I thought he was as handsome a figure of an attractive young man as I had ever seen…Franklin and I became friends – a case of love at first sight – for when men are attracted to each other there is born a feeling that Mexicans call '*simpatica*,' a word that has no counterpart in English." Daniels adopted Roosevelt as his Assistant Secretary of the Navy and became his first political sponsor. There is no doubt that Daniels' self-declared intense emotional attachment with FDR played an indispensable role in the launch of FDR's career toward the presidency. Daniels stuck with Roosevelt all the way, while also continuing a successful newspaper publishing career in North Carolina and growing a large family.

In Eleanor Roosevelt's case, the critical same-sex relationship was with Lorena Hickok (1893-1968) during FDR's 1932 campaign for president and in the touchy years of his first term, including a period when Wall Street sought a fascist military coup against them (Sally Denton, *The Plots Against the President: FDR, a Nation in Crisis and the Rise of the American Right*, 2012). The intense bond between Eleanor and Lorena, a known lesbian, propelled Eleanor to overcome her shyness and step forward as a revolutionary first lady, as documented by Maurine H. Beasley in her *Eleanor Roosevelt: Transformative First Lady* (2010). Their relationship faded by 1935, but in 1954, Eleanor helped a destitute Lorena financially by co-authoring a book with her, *Ladies of Courage* (1954).

4

The Modern Movement

A CONVERSATION I OVERHEARD ON A TRAIN from New York last week involved a very fat fundamentalist minister in shorts, and a middle aged man trying to keep up a meaningless, "manly" conversation with him. When the man debarked, he introduced his effeminate son who'd been sitting behind him having a lively, high-pitched laughter-filled conversation with a female passenger. The facial expression of the minister suddenly conveyed contempt, mostly, I'd say, for the man for failing as a parent to have "beaten the gay" out of his son. That fat, judgmental minister evoked an archetypal image of angry haters who've made life miserable for gay people from time immemorial, myself included. Such are the real bullies that young gay people suffer.

They drive fearful parents to desperate measures to de-gay their sons and daughters, with disastrous results. Gay youth suffer doubly when "cures" don't take, blamed for not trying hard enough. Love gets dashed by fear and anger, with scars that last lifetimes. Too often, youth do the suppressing on themselves, seeking acceptance and losing touch with their gay sensibilities until much later in life, if ever.

It is vital, when lacking, for gay people to get in touch with the gayness of their earliest years, to see those special gifts and sensibilities that are so often evident long before any explicitly erotic aspects come into play. There are those who just can't help but shut the bedroom door and play music to get their dance on. There are those who prefer the *accoutrements* of the gender opposite their own. There are those overloaded with empathy and compassion, who always do things for others. I preferred the company of the females among the adults and their friends in my family and I bled, emotionally, for my mother and the cruel, arbitrary conditions she endured at the hands of my father.

My innate skill was as a writer, but not in an introverted mode. Instead, I produced a newspaper, my first at age seven, which reported on news of the family and neighborhood. I went door-to-door in our little California seaside town of 300 to peddle it for a nickel. My purpose, I realized much later, was to work in legion with my mother to bring harmony to our home. (It was when I started my own newspaper, the *Falls Church News-Press*, 40 years later, that I this motivation dawned on me, and this has animated my efforts with my paper since). Yes, I loved being alone with my music in my bedroom! My favorite music was, one could say, unbeknownst to me, that of my first gay romance. It was with the music of the gay composer Peter Ilyich Tchaikovsky. Little did I know he was gay, of course, but I was all over his frilly and rich sounds and themes, and I stood in front of a mirror not dancing in the usual sense, but in the lavish manner of an orchestra conductor. I'd get goose bumps doing the *1812 Overture* or, my favorite, the final movement of his *Fifth Symphony*.

As a boy, I was known as kind and generous, and I became the best friend of a lonely Jewish boy whose mother survived the Holocaust. As a teen, I lived in the same time period and much like the gay character in Tobias Wolff's autobiographical *This Boy's Life*, the one who, in the film version, steals a kiss from the Leonardo DiCaprio character on the piano bench. I had no similar outwardly gay mannerisms, but eschewed crowds in favor of intense one-on-one friendships, and my first was with a straight lad, who I helped a lot.

High school and college days were tortuous, filled with shyness, self-loathing, acne and fear of disclosure. My newspaper talent was my only consolation. I went out for sports and struggled to date girls. Meanwhile, I lived in the same time period, again, as the high schoolers in Peter Weir's brilliant film *Dead Poets Society* set in the late 1950s. The film chronicled a precursor to the youth ferment of the 1960s, and that mood was in the air.

The only time I shared a homoerotic physical moment in all those years came when three of us, ferried by our high school English teacher, rode back from an event in Los Angeles. A girl was in the front passenger seat. A boy was with me in the back. I was very attracted to the boy, but would never act. Dozing off, I suddenly felt something. I turned to see the boy staring at me, with his warm, moist hand on my upper leg. A first, unforgettable erotic touch! But I pulled away, moaning inside even as I instantly imagined dreaded consequences of reciprocity. I couldn't break this suffocation until after college, when I did what any good gay boy would do: I enrolled in a theological seminary to find a vocation of bringing love and happiness for all.

The problem is that almost all gay history or criticism written since Stonewall in 1969 has been from the post-modern perspective, where all social reality is defined in terms of pleasure and power facets resulting in many downright errors, if not lies, concerning some basic facts.

Among the handful of notable exceptions are Rictor Norton, who in his book, *The Myth of the Modern Homosexual* (1997), systematically demolishes the post-modern so-called social constructionist dishonesty of Michel Foucault and others.

Another exception is Tennessee Williams. In Williams' case, notwithstanding those who've tried to interpret his work from the post-modern point of view, in his amazingly prolific writings from the 1960s until his death in 1983, he often wrote directly about the homosexual condition, and never let go of his signature world view defined by the polarities of cruelty and compassion, both notions rejected by post-moderns (for them, cruelty is subsumed by power and compassion by pleasure). In his late 1970s efforts like *Vieux Carre* and *Something Cloudy, Something Clear*, for example, Williams drew from his own experiences as a young homosexual to speak directly to the particular struggles of the homosexual to retain self-respect, sensitivity, integrity and creative work against the impulse of carnality-for-its-own-sake.

Such was the dominant unwritten morality of the homosexual back then, the Platonic struggle to elevate both the self and the beloved in the context of a love of beauty and creativity, against the gratification of the mere sexual act, itself. It was not so much an either/or, as a tension, to a greater or lesser degree, between the two that defined homosexual lives. Among other things, post-modernism has completely distorted essential components of gay history prior to Stonewall, painting a picture of a monolithic, linear movement that never, in fact existed that way.

The emerging early gay rights movement was an extension of the legacy of FDR and the New Deal, and pro-labor, pro-socialist currents, carried on following FDR's death by his homosexual wife, Eleanor Roosevelt, her promotion of the International Declaration of the Rights of Man through the United Nations, the Henry Wallace presidential campaign of 1948, and the likes of Tennessee Williams and Christopher Isherwood. It also had a religious component, as mainstream urban Protestant and Jewish congregations touted the progressive values of this current. In San Francisco, for example, the Council on Religion and the Homosexual forged important gains for gays in the mid-1960s, and served as the pathway for my own coming out as a seminarian.

WHAT IS VIRTUE?

IN HIS *THE PICTURE OF DORIAN Gray*, the storied homosexual Oscar Wilde (1854-1900) penned a work for popular audiences that held specific significance for his "Uranian" (the term coined by Karl Heinrich Ulrichs for homosexuals in his day) brothers and sisters. The original 1889 version had more explicit homo-eroticism than later rewrites but the message was clear, either way. Wilde made frequent forays into the urban subculture of London, to mingle among young male "panthers," hustlers and prostitutes generally the social heirs of the street urchins Charles Dickens wrote about 50 years earlier in *Oliver Twist*. From that vantage point, in *The Picture of Dorian Gray*, Wilde signaled extreme caution, warning in the way only a homosexual with first-hand experience of being entangled in such "pleasures" could, against the dismal consequences of the "New Hedonism," embodied in the philosophy of his novel's character Lord Wooton. Wilde wrote with a strong ring of truth about the dangers of groundless hedonism's descent into jaundiced depersonalization, addiction, deceit, cruelty, disease, and death.

Wilde struggled for true romance with his younger lover Bosie against the pitfalls of the the urban homosexual underworld. His was a common struggle for homosexuals. Contending with such tensions, homosexuals commonly took their satisfaction from their creative work.

In the 1950s, urban underworld culture was promoted by right-wing elements to stymie a burgeoning morally-grounded progressive movement (that included many gay pioneers). It involved a mass proliferation of LSD, elevation of Beat Poets onto a national platform, and the message of *Dorian Gray*'s hedonistic Dr. Wooten.

Gay icon Christopher Isherwood was not impressed. Isherwood, in his diaries of the 1960s published last year, wrote of meeting LSD "guru" Timothy Leary in 1967, and described him thus: "He really is a fake. The smile on his face was so slimy that you could hardly bear to look at him."

Attending a Leary "Psychedelic Celebration" the next day, Isherwood wrote, "A lot of it was ass-licking the younger generation, telling them how great they were and how free. Leary sneered at the oldlings and somehow tried to pass himself off as an honorary young man. He appealed to all the young to 'drop out, turn on, tune in,' which means, as near as you could tell, drop all obligations imposed on you by your elders, take pot, acid or whatnot and thus tune into the meaning of life. What is so false and pernicious in Leary's appeal was its complete irresponsibility. He wasn't offering any reliable spiritual help to the young, only inciting them to vaguely rebellious action, and enticing them without really involving himself with them."

Months later, in July 1967 during the so-called "Summer of Love" when hippies took over American culture, Isherwood wrote, "10,000 or maybe 100,000 hippies are expected to descend upon California in the near future, and this, say certain doctors, may start a series of epidemics, because the hippies have syphilis, gonorrhea and hepatitis." That was horribly prescient of the entire next decade, when "hippie free love" hijacked the gay liberation movement.

The June 1969 Stonewall riots, not the first involving clashes between police and gay street people (for example, the August 1966 Compton's Cafeteria riot in San Francisco), occurred at the same time as, nearby, long lines were waiting to see Mart Crowley's huge hit play, *The Boys in the Band.* That play, which began a run of 1,000 performances in January 1968, marked a high point in the civil rights-inspired current of the gay movement. It was the first of its kind to present the urban homosexual lifestyle to general audiences, and was wildly popular among gays and straights, alike. Unlike the tsunami of "sexual freedom" that later took over the movement, it was about two abiding themes: the struggle for genuine self-esteem, and the notion of a gay community.

Contrary to those who've trashed *The Boys in the Band* from the standpoint of subsequent, disingenuous postmodern hedonism, the play was not primarily about pre-liberation self-loathing. It was grounded in compassionate truth-telling, in the manner of Tennessee Williams, resonating with authenticity for gay audiences, while holding out for a far better day.

While recited as a taunt by Harold, it was actually important and liberating when the play's character told Michael, "You are a sad and pathetic man. You're a homosexual and you don't want to be. But there is nothing you can do to change it. Not all our prayers to God, not all the analysis you can buy in all the years you've got left to live. You may very well one day be able to know a heterosexual life if you want it desperately enough – if you pursue it with the fervor with which you now annihilate – but you will always be homosexual as well. Always, Michael. Always. Until the day you die."

That "affirmation" was, to me in that era, far more a clarion call to come out and to own my identity and integrity than any riot or lure of hedonistic excess. All that was missing in the lives of the characters of that play, all that was needed for their liberation, was to have them, and the wider world, understand and accept the meaning of that small speech. And finally, after all the cat fighting and drama, Harold departs by saying simply, "Call you tomorrow." The bonds in this microcosm of our wider homosexual tribe could not have been stronger, despite everything.

For a young gay man, this play made the prospect of my life as an open, and not self-loathing, homosexual not only tolerable, but expectant. It helped me to resolve, as Christopher Isherwood wrote about himself in *Christopher and His Kind* (1976), "He must never again give way to embarrassment, never deny the rights of his tribe, never apologize for its existence, never think of sacrificing himself masochistically on the altar of that false god of the totalitarians, the Greatest Good for the Greater Number – whose priests are alone empowered to decide what 'good' is." The play's characters were employed and aspiring, the way most homosexuals were who came to the big city to pursue their often enormous talents.

A CULTURE OF GREATNESS

DOMINANT GAY CULTURE REMAINS DEFINED IN that core by circuit parties, recreational drugs, mindless worship of the physical properties of certain endowed young men, boring pornography, sexual excess, the constant abuse of the emotive impulse to love by resort to casual and anonymous sex, outlandish allegedly-sexual extreme behaviors (such as "erotic vomiting," described in glowing terms in a twisted "queer theory" textbook), and the abiding popularity of Manhunt, Grindr and other casual sex hook-up sites. These features are so mainstream in gay culture today it seems hopeless, an invitation to derision, to call them into question. No wonder the yearning for something akin to normalcy among so many gays, seeking it through marriage and other institutions that parrot the even more morally-bankrupt straight society that either still hates or will never really be comfortable with them.

Kramer's character Ned Weeks in his Tony Award-winning *The Normal Heart* cries out as the reality of the AIDS epidemic unfolds, "I belong to a culture that includes Proust, Henry James, Tchaikovsky, Cole Porter, Plato, Socrates, Aristotle, Alexander the Great, Michelangelo, Leonardo da Vinci, Christopher Marlowe, Walt Whitman, Herman Melville, Tennessee Williams, Byron, E.M. Forster, Lorca, Auden, Francis Bacon, James Baldwin, Harry Stack Sullivan, John Maynard Keynes, Dag Hammarskjold… The only way we'll have real pride is when we demand recognition of a culture that isn't just sexual. It's all there – all through history we've been there; but we have to claim it, and identify who was in it, and articulate what's in our minds and hearts and all our creative contributions to this earth… That's how I want to be defined: as one of the men who fought the war. Being defined by our cocks is literally killing us. Must we all be reduced to becoming our own murderers?" That has been Larry Kramer's abiding theme.

To my mind, such a noble and heroic breed are homosexuals! We've been an indispensable glue and momentum for the maintenance and advance not only of civilization, but of civility, itself. Nature has put us here for a reason. Strip us of our rightful role, replace a zeal to create and contribute to a more just and compassionate world, reduce us to "blithe indifference," and the entire world becomes angrier, more paranoid, more selfish and cruel. Assess the wider social impact of 80,000 of the most creative souls in the world, who found their way to New York, the creative capital of the globe, to make their contribution, wiped out by AIDS, most long before they'd come close to achieving their full potential. How would the world be different today had that not happened? Would the outcome of the razor-thin 2000 presidential election in the U.S. (considered by many the most significant watershed for all the chaos that's followed) been the same? You can't remove that many homosexuals without making the world a less cheery place.

For too many who survived, the cynicism and indifference imbued into gay culture in the 1970s, and the unaddressed post-traumatic stress consequences of the AIDS era, turned them away from humanitarian ideals, to parrot their straight oppressors as harsh individualist libertarians, anarchists and jaded arch-conservatives.

Gay people will never fit in straight society. Nature provided us to transform it, not conform to it. We're meant to be neither the mindless hedonists of the urban gay culture of the 1970s, nor new Ozzie and Harriets. Nobody said this would be easy. It isn't. But we can speak to each other from the vantage point of, as Abraham Lincoln (one of us) put it, "the better angels of our nature," to love not lust, to urge one another to tackle fears and become important to the mending of an increasingly dysfunctional world."

VIRTUE VS HEDONISM

> "Virtue is rightly-ordered love."
> —St. Augustine, City of God

THE CONCEPT OF "VIRTUE," DESCRIPTIVE THROUGH history of the most highly-valued human qualities, is, truth be told, the invention of homosexuals. But it has almost disappeared from our language, a primary victim of the last 40 years' shift in social mores brought on by a counterculture that sees virtue as a primary target for destruction. Virtue, after all, centers human behavior on love, courage, consideration and justice, while anarcho-hedonist counterculture values are centered entirely on selfish self-interest. The 19th century philosopher Neitzsche ridiculed virtue, and he was a seminal influence in the post-World War II rise of the radical anarcho-hedonist movement. Tragically, anarcho-hedonism smothered the gay liberation movement in its cradle in the late 60s and early 70s, fomenting an urban gay culture of startling sexual excess, among other things, the precondition for the AIDS horror.

But the homosexuals' invention of virtue was a lawful product of our natural role in creation as ones not primarily driven by an impulse for physical species procreation, but instead for the procreation of civilization, itself. Concepts of virtue appear in the ancient writings of homosexuals Plato and Socrates who defined it as a blend of temperance, prudence, courage and justice. The Apostle Paul defines it as inclusive of "faith, hope and love" in I Corinthians 13, and in his letter to Galatians, broadens it to include love, joy, peace, patience, kindness, generosity, faithfulness, gentleness and self-control. Paul's allegedly anti-homosexual commentary in his letter to the Romans was against predatory lust, not virtuous love. St. Augustine (354-430 A.D.) defines virtue as "rightly-ordered love," consisting of all the above-mentioned qualities. Augustine is rightly included in Paul Russell's *The Gay 100* volume (1995) because he acknowledged in his autobiographical *Confessions* passionate same-sex relations as a young man. But few knew better than Augustine the consequences for civilization of wanton, out of control hedonism, being an eyewitness to the unraveling of the Roman Empire. Augustine's *City of God* was a critique of the collapsing empire, and how hedonistic rituals, including profuse homosexual acts performed by Galli priest-prostitutes, contributed to it. He observed that Rome's rulers cared not a hoot for morality, but solely for the docility of their subjects.

Like Plato and Paul, Augustine counseled restraint – or better, virtue – in cultures where massive hedonistic excess led swiftly to death, both of persons and societies. He was not anti-homosexual, but anti-dehumanizing hedonistic excess. He elevated love and virtue, with particular regard for the well-being of the beloved, over sexual hedonism. It is a challenge to see St. Augustine for who he really was in his time, and not as distorted by the cloudy prism of 1500 years of subsequent history. A critic of a crumbling civilization, he struggled to build a bastion to salvage humanity. He wrote and preached prolifically. In fact, rather than denounce virtuous same-sex intimacy, he affirmed it. He endorsed the kind of relationships we see exhibited, for example, between medieval priests played by Sean Connery and Christian Slater in the mesmerizing film version of Umberto Eco's novel, *The Name of the Rose* (1986).

The author of the poignant AIDS-era novel *Borrowed Time*, Paul Monette (1945-1995), put it in a most inspired way in his essay, *On Becoming*, in Mark Thompson's *Gay Soul: Finding the Heart of Gay Spirit and Nature* (1990). "It has been my experience," he wrote, "that gay and lesbian people who have fought through their self-hatred and their self-recriminations have a capacity for empathy that is glorious and a capacity to find a laughter in things that is like praising God. There is a kind of flagrant joy about us that goes very deep and is not available to most people." Echoing what I've affirmed in these chapters all along, he added, "Being gay is about something more profound than my sexual nature." Edmund White, in a 1991 third edition Afterword to *States of Desire*, conceded that all the 1970s "self-centered pleasure seeking…was a betrayal of an earlier philosophy that had linked homosexual rights with feminism and socialism," a passing, partially adequate reference to what I and my "Effeminist" gay activist colleagues were fighting for at that time.

Homosexual orientation, *per se*, is but one part of an individual's total distinctive personality and identity. As total persons, homosexuals are created as among the most beautiful in spirit on the planet, who bring important, unique gifts. Without us around, humanity suffers. We're naturally generated as a portion of the universe's evolution designed to bring unique features necessary for the ultimately harmonious unfolding of life. Same-sex erotic attraction is but one manifestation of the homosexual's total complement of special gifts. Others I have described as a heightened sense of empathy that can be called gay sensibility an alternate sensual perspective, and a constructive nonconformity.

The straight world is not entirely devoid of these qualities. On the contrary, it is our purpose as homosexuals, working with the social emancipation of women, to heighten these qualities for civilization as a whole. But we homosexuals gain from appreciating that they constitute the core of our total personhood, that they are our tribal identity, so to speak. Our natural adversary is the tyrant, the tyrannies great and small derived from unchallenged straight male dominion. That domination is over women, children and subjugated peoples, and derived territorial and resource perceived requirements that cause wars. That is how nature, in its human social form, is organized – 93 percent of it, roughly, that is.

We, homosexuals, are that percent that stands in the way of male dominion's total lust for conquest and control. We liberate the oppressed, as our great poet laureate Walt Whitman wrote, "The attitude of great poets [that's us!] is to cheer up slaves and horrify despots" (*Leaves of Grass*). We attend to the widows and orphans, we construct and operate the institutions of mercy and fairness. We emancipate abused women and boys whose fathers train them to fight and die in their wars or become their dulled corporate clones. Because we are homosexual, we are not obsessed with species reproduction and territorial dominion but have an alternative sensual perspective directed more to beauty and forms that elevate and humanize the spirit. When a straight brute walks into a room, he orients immediately, in his constant urge to reproduce, to any attractive women there. When a gay person walks into the same room, he or she orients instead toward whether the drapes and the carpet match.

In terms of constructive nonconformity, we are challenged to recognize that we will never, nor should, fit in to male-dominated society, but that it is in our very core to counter its influence in a myriad of ways – from camp and acting out, to public service, scientific discovery, invention, education, design and higher art in myriad forms. These are all ways in which "constructive nonconformity" gets expressed, and the natural impulse of the unbridled straight male is always threatened by this at one or another level. When emancipated women and gays rule the world, we will impose a lasting, if uneasy, peace that will eventually evolve into a more humane, enlightened and productive species.

Our great genius Oscar Wilde (1854-1900), brought down from the heights of fame and celebrity to humiliation and shunning when convicted of the "the love that dare not speak its name" (homosexuality), wrote a letter from prison in 1897 entitled *De Profundis*. The first part directed to his beloved Alfred Douglas ("Bosie"), its second part counts among the magnificent short works in literature. Wilde's remorse was not for being gay, or for the "crime" for which he was convicted, but for the arrogance that ignored the consequences of flagrant behavior, which by ruining him, ruined his benefit to humanity. "Sorrow," he wrote, " is the supreme emotion of which man is capable," adding "I must say to myself that I ruined myself and that nobody great or small can be ruined except by his own hand." Wilde referred to "the fierce misery of those who live for pleasure." Then he wrote of "that imaginative sympathy in the entire sphere of human relations, which is the sole secret of creation." Male chauvinist civilization's great vice is arrogance, a wanton disregard for the consequences of behavior on general social well-being. In our "Age of Contagion," homosexuals aped that arrogance. Through contrition comes a restart.

It was by a remarkable and gracious coincidence that the first weekend after the passing of our gay movement's greatest pioneer, Franklin Kameny, in October 2011, the Martin Luther King Jr. Memorial was dedicated on the National Mall. The ceremony included a viewing of the entirety of Dr. King's 17-minute "I Have a Dream" speech delivered on the steps of the Lincoln Memorial to 300,000 in the "Great March on Washington" of August 28, 1963, the year of the 100th anniversary of Lincoln's signing of the Emancipation Proclamation.

Seven of the handful of original gay members of the Mattachine Society of Washington, led by Kameny, attended that historic rally and heard that speech. It was with its echoes ringing in their ears that in 1965, Kameny and a tiny cadre of fellow homosexuals carried out the first-ever organized picket line demanding homosexual equality held at the White House gates. In his 1963 speech, Dr. King welcomed the racially-diverse makeup of the rally. "Many of our white brothers, as evidenced by their presence here today, have come to realize that their destiny is tied up with our destiny. They have come to realize that their freedom is inextricably bound to our freedom," he intoned. "We hold these truths to be self-evident: that all men are created equal," Dr. King declared. "I have a dream that my four little children will one day live in a nation where they will not be judged by the color of their skin but by the content of their character."

That speech directly inspired the rise of our modern gay movement, led by Kameny (May 21, 1925-October 11, 2011), Lilli Vincenz, Barbara Gittings and a handful of others, as chronicled in the film documentary, *Gay Pioneers* (2004), produced by the Philadelphia Equality Forum. Frank Kameny, I am proud to say, was my friend in recent years. He was arguably the single most seminal influence in the history of our movement, as claimed at a Rainbow History Project forum. Kameny was scheduled to speak at that forum before his untimely death at age 86 just two days before. His was the strident, compelling force that led the effort against the 1950s McCarthyite anti-homosexual witch hunts in the government (David K. Johnson, *The Lavender Scare: The Cold War Persecution of Gays and Lesbians in the Federal Government*, 2004). He organized picket lines when no one else was doing it and carried on a relentless, lifelong fight for equality. He ran for public office and railed loudly against injustice in an era when no one, except in rarefied circles of literary or artistic elites, dared publicly declare their homosexuality.

His crowning achievement was his relentless, eventually successful campaign to get the American Psychiatric Association to remove homosexuality from its list of mental disorders in 1973. That signal achievement changed the public perception of homosexuality, laying the groundwork for growing public acceptance and affirmation since. Kameny invented the slogan, "Gay is Good," far more controversial in its time than it seems now. I defended it then against objections of dedicated gay friends who considered it too radical.

When I first met Frank, I was a young gay activist in 1970 in San Francisco. Dr. King's speech permeating the national ethos, I'd made two life-changing decisions, entering seminary in 1966 and joining Kameny and his San Francisco counterparts prior to Stonewall in early 1969 to come out and join the struggle for gay, and human, liberation. Our fight, I wrote in the editorial for the first *Gay Sunshine* newspaper, "should harken to a greater cause, the cause of human liberation, of which homosexual liberation is just one aspect." Regrettably, about that same time, the onslaught of the right wing, socially-engineered anarcho-hedonist counterculture hijacked our movement, dashing Dr. King's appeal to the "content of character" in the process. We've had to live, and die, with the consequences of that since.

I reconnected with Frank in recent years, while his contributions became more recognized and appreciated. A milestone came when the many picket signs, leaflets, speeches and photographs he'd kept from his earliest activist days were formally received as a special collection at the Smithsonian Institution. He was honored at the White House by President Obama, and a photo of him and me with Vice President Biden hangs in my office.

Along with another other early activist and mutual friend, Lilli Vincenz, and her long-time partner Nancy Davis, I hosted Frank as my guest at the national dinner of the Human Rights Campaign in 2005, and often invited him to lunches at The Palm restaurant in downtown D.C.

Those many lunches were not only to enjoy his company, but to provide opportunities for my friends, especially younger ones, gay and otherwise, to meet and appreciate this genuine hero of our movement. Recently, of this "Gay Science" project of mine, Kameny smiled and quipped, "I think we wind up in the same place." I concurred.

I am treating the issues of our gay identity, new (or, very ancient) gay morality and our future from the standpoint of the American revolutionary promise of "life, liberty and the pursuit of happiness." On liberty, I take the liberty of substituting "liberation." Also, it is noted that the phrase, "pursuit of happiness," wound up in the "Declaration of Independence" over objections from some who wanted "property" there instead. "The pursuit of happiness," by contrast to property, is at the heart of what the American experience is intended to be. Not happiness, mind you, but the pursuit of it. The American notion of the democratic republic, and how it has progressed against all odds toward the achievement of its founding goals, grounded as it is in the affirmation that "all are created equal," has among its greatest progenitors in history, us!

It is worth examining this history, as I have in this series, as a form of self-discovery of what it really means to be gay, a member of the LGBT tribe. We are that indispensable component of creation and civilization, that nature's purpose has provided to engineer the highest, most noble aspirations and inspirations, and to translate those into modes of just and compassionate governing. In this current, government becomes the will of the people behaving collectively on the basis of universal principles of fairness, justice and provision for the opportunity of all to attain their fullest potentials.

Naturally, we are not the only ones who embody all this, as it is precisely our purpose and our success to spread it far and wide. But there is this special role for us, we who are empowered to love in a Platonic manner, rather than being driven by natural erotic impulses primarily to reproduce the species. I have looked at the history and impact of our tribe from this point of view, seeing the imprint of our influence on history in these forms, and not from today's popular historical reductionism and shallow empirical investigations into evidence of mere sexual activity. But two misguided tangents grip our cause in ways we can see more clearly now than in the fog of the Age of Contagion and its aftermath. The first is society's pressure on us to "assimilate," to be clones of today's dominant, banal consumerist culture, and it's understandable to want that, given our history of repression and pain. The second is the unproductive reaction against that in a modern variant of anarcho-hedonism.

Photos

Nicholas Benton (right) in 1959, from his yearbook in the 9th grade as the founder and editor of his homeroom newspaper with his first very best friend, Allen.

AUTHOR BENTON (left) in his Effeminist counterculture days, 1970, with companion Bobby.

With then, in 2009, Vice President and now President Joe Biden (center), author Nicholas Benton (right) and fellow gay pioneer Frank Kameny.

In 2016, Benton (left) with gay icon, the late Larry Kramer (center), and Benton's friend Simon VanSteyn (right).

In 2019 with Don Bachardy (right), long-time companion of the late author Christopher Isherwood. Bachardy and Isherwood rented a house from Benton's aunt, whom they admired, in the Santa Monica canyon in the 1950s.

Nicholas Benton on the occasion of the 30th anniversary in 2021 of his founding the Washington, D.C.-area progressive general interest newspaper, the *Falls Church News-Press*.

5

Conceived in the Shadow
of Tennessee Williams

THE TOUCHSTONE FOR MY WORK IS an article by James
Grauerholz in the May 16, 1977 *Village Voice* that involved
a conversation between Tennessee Williams and William
Burroughs. In the summer of 2010, I was at my condominium
pool reading *Conversations With Tennessee Williams* (1986),
an anthology edited by Albert J. Devlin, when I stumbled
onto it, and a light went off, more like a nuclear explosion,
in my head. My own understanding as an early gay pioneer
and of the subsequent unfolding of the movement, including
the AIDS crisis, suddenly broke forth with angelic music. I
quoted the exchange earlier in this book. In it, Williams is
stunned to discover that Burroughs repudiates the notion
that there is any such thing as "right" or "wrong" in human
behavior. The depths of Burroughs' nihilism and amorality
genuinely startled Williams, and I recalled afresh the powerful
influence of Burroughs' worldview in the early gay liberation
movement (cited at the beginning of Chapter 2 above).

There were three trends that fed into the gay liberation movement in the post-Stonewall era. The first was the colorful, courageous and enormously talented work of Williams and Isherwood (my favorites) and early founders of the gay movement, including my friends, the late Frank Kameny and Lilli Vincenz and others aligned more broadly with the causes of civil rights and justice.

The second was entirely different, a 1960's countercultural paradigm shift fueled by radical anarcho-hedonist theory and practice, expounding "sex, drugs and rock-and-roll." This "revolution" repudiated the progressive values-based work of earlier periods in favor of postmodern and post-structural nihilism and radical hedonism. Ginsberg, Burroughs and others fell into this current, which had an influential and ultimate cynic as a leader, Michel Foucault.

The third current was made up of those of us who saw "gay liberation" as a world-historical opportunity to assert a new offensive against the male-dominated cultural paradigm, including its preoccupation with the subjugation of women, children, workers and other exploited peoples in its lust for expanding territories through tyranny and war.

We aligned with radical feminists and for want of a better term, called ourselves "effeminists." We drew on the tradition of the earlier gay movement, seeing ourselves as its new cutting edge.

But the anarcho-hedonists swept like a tsunami over the gay movement. Free and frequent impersonal sex was not only sanctioned in urban centers, it became a veritable imperative. Anyone preferring romance and respect for persons was assailed as "sex negative."

In this context, I observe these things about Christopher Bram's *Eminent Outlaws: The Gay Writers Who Changed America* (2012). First, Winston Leyland did not "found" *Gay Sunshine*, the nation's first gay liberation-based alternative newspaper, in 1970. It was founded by a collective in which Leyland was a member, as was I. I wrote the editorial for that newspaper's first edition, quoted in part in Don Teal's *The Gay Militants* (1971). If the collective had any leader, it was Konstantin Berlandt (1946-1994). After the first few editions, Leyland effectively hijacked *Gay Sunshine* from the collective against its will, something not hard to do in those disheveled days. Second, Bram's contention that "gay liberation did not create gay promiscuity" does not take into account the anarcho-hedonist paradigm shift, which changed the very nature of promiscuity. Third, writing about the first news of AIDS, Bram states "In terms of what was known about the illness at the time, (Larry) Kramer was overreacting. Yet he turned out to be right." That odd contradiction is the popular dig at Kramer. How can someone be "overreacting" when he is "right?" Fourth, Bram says of Tennessee Williams' death that he had "died as a writer" years earlier. This conventional wisdom is now being challenged by Williams scholars who are finding tremendous creativity in Williams' later works, including one he was working on at his death, *In Masks Outrageous and Austere*. It was not Williams who changed, or declined, but the wider culture, no longer interested in his compassionate truth-telling. It became far too jaded to appreciate him.

The powerful influence on American culture by prominent post-World War II gay authors, as documented in *Eminent Outlaws*, raises the question of just how they contributed to the explosion of the modern gay liberation movement, when countless people burst out of their closets more forcefully and openly than any of those authors had, at least up to that point in the late 1960s. After all, for most of them – the likes of Tennessee Williams, Christopher Isherwood, Truman Capote, Gore Vidal, James Baldwin and others – references to gay issues were very muted, at best, in their popular works.

How, then, did they impact someone like myself, born near the end of World War II, growing up in the 1950s in a remote community, never knowingly encountering another gay person, entering graduate seminary in Berkeley, Calif., in the late 1960s and suddenly bursting out of my closet to co-found the Berkeley Gay Liberation Front? Surely, I was influenced by Tennessee Williams' famous plays. But I learned only later how much closer to their influence I actually was, and how one movie by two members of their inner circle actually changed my life.

My title, *Conceived in the Shadow of Tennessee Williams*, is more than metaphor. In Williams' extensive diaries, his fascinating 828-page *Notebooks* published in 2006, he wrote lavishly about his gay experiences. Cavorting among young soldiers during nightly blackouts (precautionary measures throughout the West Coast against the prospect of a Japanese attack) on the palisades above Santa Monica brought him very close, geographically, to me. On Sept. 12, 1943, he wrote, "The unprecedented sex activity continues. The night that I don't desecrate the little god all over again is exceptional." There were expressions of remorse: sex, he wrote, "is about like a dog pissing on a tree," adding on Sept. 26, "I have accepted sex as a way of life and found it empty, empty knuckles on a hollow drum." But on Nov. 15 he reported "a record for me of five times perfectly reciprocal pleasure." While he was doing all this on the palisades, often bringing men to his modest dwelling, I was busy being conceived in the Santa Monica below. Thus the title for this chapter. Could a rag from one of Tennessee's trysts have floated down off the palisades and magically impregnated my mom such that Williams is my real father? Haha!

This happened at almost the same time that Williams and Isherwood met for the first time, the beginning of a very long friendship. Isherwood's diaries also revealed a surprisingly immediate brush with my world. He and his young partner Don Bachardy (now, at age 86, my friend) rented a house from my Aunt Ginny in Santa Monica, and he wrote about her. Writing on May 28, 1955, he called her "Ms. Hoerner," she being my dad's older sister and a frequent visitor to our home in Santa Barbara, a two-hour drive away, where I'd just turned 11. "Yesterday morning, I talked to Mrs. Hoerner," Isherwood wrote. "She tells me she is looking for a Buddha. She wants to put it in a shrine and light incense sticks in front of it. The Buddha she has now is unsatisfactory, but she burns the incense, just the same; and if she's out, her son Griff does it – although he squirms if ever she talks about religion."

"We got to know her well," Don Bachardy told me. "I can still remember the sound of her voice." He noted that Isherwood "took an interest in her son," my first cousin Griff.

In his diary, Isherwood wrote, "Griff is nearly seventeen, and the other day she found he'd started flying lessons without her permission. Eleven dollars a lesson – he makes the money by washing cars." Griff carried his passion for flying throughout his life, giving flight lessons for a living before dying in an accident doing that in 2010. Aunt Ginny commented years later about the wild parties Isherwood and Bachardy threw. The diaries chronicled the many luminaries who attended. Ginny was extraordinary, clairvoyant, and my principal correspondent after I became a gay activist in San Francisco in 1970 and was banished, consequently, from my family by my father, her brother.

In the early 1960s, I was the same age and traversed the same turf as Isherwood's character, Kenny, in his novel, *A Single Man* (1964), played by Nicholas Hoult in the movie version (2009). A college student in Santa Barbara, I played baseball on the same Los Angeles campus and at the same time identified in that story. Those days, I'd vowed to take my gay secret to the grave. But then I saw a life-changing film, written by William Inge and directed by Elia Kazan, both tight in the Isherwood-Williams circles, *Splendor in the Grass*. It had a transformative impact with a bang in the case of what Inge's film, *Splendor in the Grass*, did to me. It was a powerful punch to my psychic gut like none I've experienced before or since. It contributed to big decisions I made and the world view I carried with me my entire adult life, informing of my contributions to the gay liberation movement among other things.

The American playwright William Inge (1913-1973) was so tight with Tennessee Williams that scholars speculate they might have been lovers at some point. He was in the intimate gay literary circles of Williams, Christopher

Isherwood, Gore Vidal and others, and among the most successful, winning a Pulitzer Prize for his 1953 play, *Picnic*, and an Academy Award for his 1961 film, *Splendor in the Grass*. But Christopher Bram mostly overlooks Inge in *Eminent Outlaws: Gay Writers Who Changed America* and generally Inge has not enjoyed the same stature as his gay literary colleagues of that era, possibly because he insisted on remaining more closeted than they were. The important interconnections between Inge, Williams and the others ("Williams and His Contemporaries: William Inge", the transcript of a panel moderated by Annette Saddik at the 2006 Tennessee Williams Scholars' Conference) helps define the impact all these great literary figures had collectively on post-World War II American culture. Tennessee Williams brought a similar theme to his earliest and most important explicit contribution to the early gay liberation dialogue (in his play, *Small Craft Warnings*, 1972), confirming that Inge's work was an offspring of discourses within those tight gay literary circles of the 1950s.

Inge's screenplay for *Splendor in the Grass* combined with Elia Kazan's direction and a young Natalie Wood's acting to produce a classic cultural intervention into the numbing routine of life in America in the 1950s and early 1960s. It set millions of teenagers, including myself, pondering the correlation between growing into conformity with the adult values of a dull yet savage society and the quashing of the idealistic passions of youth.

The characters of Wilma Dean (Natalie Wood) and Bud (Warren Beatty) were passionate high school sweethearts in a small town in Inge's home state of Kansas about the same age as Inge was in 1928-29 when the story took place, subsuming the great stock market crash of October 1929.

The long and short of the story is contained in its title, a line from a lengthy poem by English poet William Wordsworth (1770-1850) "Ode: Imitations of Immortality" from *Recollections of Early Childhood* (1807):

> What though the radiance which was once so
>   bright
> Be now forever taken from my sight,
> Though nothing can bring back the hour
> Of splendor in the grass, of glory in the flower
> We will grieve not, rather find
> Strength in what remains behind;
> In the primal sympathy
> Which having been must ever be...

In the movie, the power and passion of Wilma Dean's and Bud's young love is beaten down by convention and parental expectations, ripping them apart, driving Deanie to a mental institution and Bud, pressured by his father, to Yale. The market crash wiping out his father's fortune, Bud returns to Kansas married to a pizza parlor waitress he met in college to work a small farm. Deanie leaves the mental institution after two and a half years and, coming home, decides to look in on Bud. She hides her surprise at discovering Bud's wife and young child. "Are you happy, Bud?," Deanie asks in monotone. "I guess so. I don't ask myself that question very much," Bud replies. "I don't think too much about happiness, either," Deanie then says, and Bud responds, "You have to take what comes." That was it.

I was deeply troubled by that film, and can remember coming home to take a very long look at myself in the living room mirror. I had no words to verbalize my feeling, but I have come to realize that my resolve from that night was to not allow the deadening of the human spirit I had just witnessed to happen to me. Little did I know it was the gay literary circle of Williams, Isherwood, Inge and others that had just drilled down into my gay soul. If a life of monotony and passionless mediocrity was to be the fate of most people as they grew out of their childhood idealism, it would be even more deadly to a closeted gay boy, pressured to conform in those ways to cover up and deny himself to himself and everybody else. As my life had begun to trend toward that kind of mediocrity, it soon began to take a dramatically different course. Settled as I was in my hometown, with a solid career ahead and assurances by my powerful boss that I would not be drafted for Vietnam, instead I decided to leave for a graduate theological seminary in Berkeley, California.

All three major players in this project, the gay but closeted Inge, Kazan and Wood, were tight in the circles of the eminent gay writers of that era, generally orbiting around the life-long friendship of Tennessee Williams and Christopher Isherwood. Kazan directed Williams' classic *A Streetcar Named Desire* and other triumphs, and Wood was among the many fine performers such as Elizabeth Taylor who often preferred the company of such gay geniuses. In fact, Wood's closest personal aide, the gay Mart Crowley, went on to write the screenplay for the first major Broadway

(1968) and film (1970) play devoted entirely to the urban gay lifestyle of that period, *Boys in the Band*. It's a little-known fact that Crowley appeared in drag in a brief cameo role in the final scene of *Splendor in the Grass* as one of the girls driving the truck carrying the Wood character away from the farm of her once-passionate lover.

The friendship between Williams and Isherwood is a fascinating study in its own right, if only because both gay men as prolific writers devoted great energy to keeping diaries, published only many years after their deaths. Both diaries recorded, from their differing standpoints, the time that the two first met in Santa Monica, California, in 1943. Williams' diary was published as *Notebooks: Tennessee Williams* in 2006. In there, on May 23, 1943, Williams wrote, "I met Christopher Isherwood. Liked him, he was so much as I had thought he would be. But he has ignored me since the one meeting, in spite of a letter I sent him. It was foolishly done, the letter."

Isherwood's diary has been published as two volumes so far, going to the end of the 1960s. In the first volume, *Diaries, Volume One, 1939-1960*, published in 1996, he wrote of meeting Williams for the first time. Dated May 13, 1943, the entry read, "Yesterday I had lunch with Tennessee Williams, the writer. He's a strange boy, small, plump and muscular, with a slight cast in one eye; full of amused malice. He has a job with Metro. He wanted to buy an autoglide to ride to work on. I tried to dissuade him, but he insisted. We went to a dealer's, and he selected a very junky old machine which is obviously going to give trouble."

Much later, in 1972 Williams first published his *Memoirs*, his major, general public-directed "coming out" life testament. It appeared in the midst of the early, most explosive period of the modern gay liberation movement, and in it he wrote again of meeting Isherwood in 1943, "We became great friends. We used to go out on the pier at Santa Monica for fish dinners. This was during World War II when almost everything was blacked out. There was an almost sentimental attachment between us but it didn't come to romance: instead, it turned into a great friendship, one of the continuing friendships of my life, and one of the most important ones." Nearby at the same time, as I reported earlier, I was being conceived by my parents.

In his *Memoirs*, Williams wrote from his heart, more concerned for that than any memory lapses or deviations from his own earlier diaries. But he identified four features of his personality as a youth that I can directly relate to from my own life, and perhaps holds for many other gays, as well. First, he suffered a "phobia about the process of thought." He wrote, "Abruptly, it occurred to me that the process of thought was a terrifyingly complex mystery of human life." He called it, "The terrifying nature of cerebration," which was lifted from him as if by a miracle as a teen and never returned. Secondly, he wrote, "My adolescent problems took their most violent form in a shyness of a pathological degree....I developed the habit of blushing whenever anyone looked me in the eyes....I don't think I had effeminate mannerisms but somewhere deep in my nerves there was an imprisoned young girl." Thirdly, he had an "early childhood disposition to his art."

Fourthly, he held a belief in God, though not of religion or ceremony. He wrote. "I have never doubted the existence of God nor have I ever neglected to kneel in prayer when a situation in which I found myself (and there have been many) seemed critical enough in my opinion to merit the Lord's attention and, I trust, intervention."

In a century defined by the most savage of brutal wars and genocides, among those things that legendary gay writers Tennessee Williams and Christopher Isherwood held in common were their pacifist political sensibilities and remarkable attention to their creative work, despite innumerable distractions, to express them. Williams wrote in Memoirs that he voted only once for president, for the perennial socialist/pacifist candidate Norman Thomas in 1932. But through his works he contributed to the rise of the civil rights, anti-war and gay liberation movements of the 1960s, as well as the elections of John F. Kennedy and Lyndon Johnson, and he was fully aware of his role in these effects. (If 400,000 gays had not died of AIDS after that, how might American electoral history be different?).

The British-born Isherwood (1904-1986) was an eyewitness to Hitler's thuggish rise to power in Berlin that forced him to leave. Isherwood suffered as his first true love, Heinz Neddermeyer, fled, was arrested and forced to join Hitler's army. Isherwood came to New York in 1939, and when he applied for U.S. citizenship in 1945, he filled out his application saying he would "defend his country" in non-combatant roles only. He became a devout follower of the pacifist Vedanta faith, and his diaries show that from the time he met the 18-year-old who was to become his life partner, Don Bachardy, in 1953 until his death in 1986, Isherwood's spirituality played a big role in his ability to hold his relationship together through stormy times and despite the great difference in their ages, while helping Bachardy develop his own considerable artistic talent. Bachardy, now 78 and a friend, was the subject of countless entries in Isherwood's diaries, dedicated to him.

Williams' pacifism was expressed against the brutality of society overall, focusing on the microcosmic male chauvinist violence of which great wars are a predicate. He characterized prevailing culture as "a society whose elite was so grossly affluent, I mean a society that numbered its billions of dollars as he counted our nickels…a nation ruled by that numerically tiny gang which has fitted itself on the top of the totem pole and is scared of getting dizzy if it glances down on…our Babylonian plutocracy." The impact of the structural brutality of culture on the weak and sensitive forms the core of most of Williams' works, including as driven by the horror of experiencing his own sister subjected to the widespread practice in those days, a lobotomy.

Williams worked tirelessly, formulating new experiments to assail the evils and injustices of such brutalities until the day he died accidentally in a New York hotel room in February 1983.

The play that he completed while writing his *Memoirs* in 1972, *Small Craft Warnings*, was dedicated to "a good many other young writers and/or artists" like him, all "disregarding the small craft warnings" while sailing into the teeth of a brutal and indifferent society. He cited the case of "such a tremendous yet fragile artist as Hart Crane," one "small craft" that crashed. The only possession Williams carried with him when he plucked chickens in Southern California and went to Mexico in the Depression-ridden late 1930s was a book of poems by the closeted gay American poet Crane (1899-1932). The subject of a new movie, *The Broken Tower*, Crane, brilliant and an optimist in his poetry, committed suicide after being rebuffed and beaten by a sailor during a cruise in the Gulf of Mexico. Williams was greatly influenced by Crane in his own poetry, and, as he declared in remarks he'd prepared for delivery the morning after he tragically died, insofar as he thought of all his work as, most fundamentally, poetry.

As Plato wrote, "Poetry is nearer to vital truth than history."

Don Bachardy recounted to me about Williams' great triumph, the Pulitzer Prize-winning *Cat on a Hot Tin Roof* (1955). It opened in Philadelphia prior to moving to Broadway. Williams invited Isherwood and Bachardy to the opening. On the eve of the first performance, he invited them to his hotel suite, and did a one-man reading of the entire play, changing his voice for each of the different characters. Bachardy said that he's seen the play performed a half dozen times since, including the 1958 film version, but he's never seen it done as well as Williams did it that night.

Williams was limited in his plays to discrete references of off-stage gay tragedies, such as in *A Streetcar Named Desire* where his character Blanche tells of having married "a boy who wrote poetry" and "thought him almost too fine to be human," but then found out, "this beautiful and talented young man was a degenerate." She confronted him cruelly, and he committed suicide. Then, 25 years later in his *Small Craft Warnings*, Williams again portrayed an off-stage sensitive and talented youth who suffered the same fate, although in this play, there were also explicit homosexual references and characters. It is likely that Williams had in mind in these references the sensitive young gay American poet whose work he so admired who had committed suicide in 1932, Hart Crane.

Prior to 1975, while Isherwood alluded to gay figures in his *Goodbye to Berlin* and other works, it was never in connection with either himself as the presumptive narrator, or his main characters.

In *Christopher and His Kind*, he went back to diaries and letters in the late 1920s and 1930s to show how he had cloaked his gay relationships in his works from that period. Isherwood was, among other things, able to enlighten us with the amazing continuity that ran from E.M. Forster (1879-1970), author of *Maurice* (written in 1913 but not published until after Stonewall in 1971) and his friend, a pioneering theorist of the unique role of gay sensibility in culture, Edward Carpenter (1844-1929), through him, his associations and to the present, his still-active long-time companion, Don Bachardy.

In it, Isherwood wrote of his efforts to compose a novel about Berlin in 1932 he called *The Lost*, the title operating on three levels: the first, he wrote, being "those who have lost their own way, that mass of Germans who were now being herded blindly into the future by their Nazi shepherds." Second were "the doomed," those "already marked down as Hitler's victims," and, third were "those whom respectable society regards as moral outcasts." He cited an entry from his diary then: "The link which binds all the chief characters together is that in some way or other, each one of them is conscious of the mental, economic, and ideological bankruptcy of the world in which they live. And all this must echo and re-echo the refrain: It can't go on like this. I'm the lost, we're the Lost." It was eventually published as *The Last of Mr. Norris* (1935).

Much is contained in Christopher Isherwood's classic memoir, *Christopher and His Kind*, which speaks directly to the matters of gay identity and purpose that have been the subject of this series. His formidable works written in the tumultuous era from the late 1920s to the onset of World War II contain enormously beneficial insights into the dehumanizing horrors of tyrannical extremism in that era taking the form of national regimes, fascists in Germany, Italy and Spain, Stalinists in the U.S.S.R. Isherwood's contributions were to the good of humankind as a whole, written in a literary form that was not preachy, not succumbing to parroting the popular political rhetoric of the time, although there is no doubt that his sentiments were, if not entirely pro-Communist, at least fervently anti-fascist.

Many, many years later, after World War II, after the civil rights and anti-war ferment of the 1960s in the U.S. (born in England, Isherwood moved to the U.S. in 1939 and never left), after the rise of the modern gay liberation movement surrounding the Stonewall riots of 1969, Isherwood revealed in *Christopher and His Kind* the indispensable ways in which his homosexuality was at the heart of his efforts at benefiting the wider human community.

Indeed, his affirmation early in life to "live according to my nature, and to find a place where I can be what I am" was fundamental to everything he did. Each of us helps humanity best, he wrote, "by using his own weapons." For him his best weapon was obviously writing, but it was also the perspective he brought by virtue of being openly and self-assuredly gay. His alternate perspective explained why he became a pacifist on the eve of World War II, he wrote, even as all the horrors of tyranny and genocide swirled around. It was because, he thought, he had so deeply loved Heinz, a man who'd been forced to join Hitler's army, that he could not bring himself to destroy a unit that might have his lover in it. Then, by extrapolation, "Because every man in that Army could be somebody's Heinz…I have no right to play favorites." Here, an expression of gay sensibility, of same-sex erotic attraction, arises in society as nature's indispensable antidote to the insanity of war. Indeed, nature provides for and sets apart gay sensibility for just such purposes.

"How could I have dare suggest," Isherwood wrote, "that any of these people – or any people anywhere – ought to fight, ought to die in defense of any principles, however excellent? I must honor those who fight of their own free will…and I must try to imitate their courage by following my path as a pacifist, wherever it takes me." Here, the same-sex lover seeks to intervene on behalf of the life and happiness of all of his sex.

Nature provides no one else to do this, at least not without the force of such a nudge. Fathers groom their sons for war. Mothers obey their husbands. State leaders give the marching orders. Bands play. Everyone cheers, and the young, rosy cheeked youths of countless nations march off seeking glory, and finding unspeakable pain, fear, the devastation of their souls and inglorious death. But the gay person is positioned by nature to defy that order from the very core of his nature. He loves those soldiers too much. He hears the echoes in his soul of the Biblical confession, "By the grace of God, I am what I am," and the affirmation, "Love that to which you are inclined. But I really love it, with everything that entails. Don't exploit it, don't rape it, don't devour and abandon it, but love it." This is why the paradigmatic straight male and his institutions – the "Others," in Isherwood's words – will always hate and seek to inflict harm on us, we, in Isherwood's words, of "Our Tribe," we homosexuals.

6

American Roots

I HAVE UNDERTAKEN THIS PROJECT DRAWING ON a number
of aspects, the overarching being the integrity of my
identity as a gay man throughout my adult life, including
my accomplishments as a pro-civil rights post-graduate
theological seminary honor graduate inspired by Dr. Martin
Luther King, a journalist (something of an innate inclination
ranging from my first newspaper at age 7 to my last 20
years founding, owning and editing a weekly newspaper),
historian, and, in terms of the gay movement, four years of
pioneering activism from before Stonewall in 1969 to 1973.

During my gay activist phase, coming out in the spirit
of Dr. King's admonition to stand tall such that no one can
hold you down following my graduation from seminary,
I became a pioneer in the founding of the *Gay Sunshine*
newspaper, authoring its first editorial, an official spokesman
for the gay movement at an anti-Vietnam War rally, a regular
contributor to the *Berkeley Barb* alternative weekly and gay-
themed papers and, with Jim Rankin, the founder of *The
Effeminist*, a combination newspaper and faction in the gay

movement. I was keenly aware of how the "sex, drugs and rock-and-roll" counterculture that was mainstreamed into American culture in the late 1960s swept the gay movement shortly after Stonewall with a blizzard of "sexual freedom" mandates, forcibly brushing away any efforts, including my own, at realizing the potential of the movement for transforming the identity and self-esteem of gays and being a positive force for wider social change.

The Effeminist effort involved arguing for gay men to align politically with the goals of the feminist movement to overthrow the influence of the brutal straight male paradigm dominating society in favor of a new paradigm based on genuine gender, racial and cultural equality.

I wrote about our "Effeminism" current in an essay included in a collection published by City Lights Books in 2010 entitled, *Smash the Church, Smash the State! The Early Years of Gay Liberation* (Tommi Avicolli Mecca, editor). My entry was entitled, "Berkeley and the Fight for an Effeminist, Socially Transformative Gay Identity."

In the same volume, reflecting the transcontinental influence of the current, Steven F. Dansky wrote a piece entitled, "The Effeminist Movement." In my essay, I included excerpts from a piece I wrote in October 1970 in *Gay Sunshine* on the "sociocultural revolution embedded in the very notion of gay liberation." I wrote, "Sex between persons of the same sex is the cultural antithesis to the most fundamental proposition of the whole Western capitalist mentality, which is derived from one fundamental act, the 'missionary position' (male atop female) sexual intercourse." I continued, "The 'missionary position,' penis in vagina for the explicit purpose of the creation of offspring, is the first presupposition of everything Western civilization represents. From it are derived the concepts of purposeful existence, patriarchy, capitalism, nationalism, imperialism, fascism. From it come the thought patterns of active/ passive, dominant/submissive, I/you, we/they, top/bottom, greater/lesser, win/lose and on and on and on…An absolute antithesis of this presupposition is an orgasmic sexual act between persons of the same sex."

In the summer of 1971, Rankin and I "developed the notion of the social paradigm shift that we felt gay liberation represented," I wrote in my essay. "We saw the movement aligned with radical feminism as an effort to end the war and oppression by transforming male-dominated society. To this end, we argued against those who saw gay liberation as only sexual freedom, or even as strictly a fight for legal rights. Many of my articles in the *Berkeley Barb* promoted the notion that, fully actualized, gay liberation had the potential to be socially transformative."

But the "sexual freedom" faction crushed us, and the rest is history, until now. On my "exile" from the gay movement in 1973 until I launched the corporate structure for my newspaper, the *Falls Church News-Press*, in 1987, I will say only this: My decision to align my life with a strident, tightly-knit, pro-socialist configuration, if nothing else, saved my life. I struggled with demons by studying classics and advocating in remote places for ways to relieve droughts and feed the world.

I remember the moment when someone came into my office in July 1981 waving a newspaper to announce the news of a "gay cancer." An electric bolt shot through me and I immediately feared the worst. It turned out far worse than I could have imagined. In 1985, I landed in the hospital with nonspecific symptoms, and feared I had AIDS, a death sentence. It turned out not to be so. That, the development of a test for HIV antibodies (I tested negative) and the moral wheels having come off my associations by their exploitation of homophobia for political gain, compelled my emphatic break, with prejudice. I proceeded to do what any good gay boy would do. I put my talents for the public good by starting a newspaper.

This series is not as a history, or a memoir, but an argument, a case for a better perception of gay identity, based on evidence that far from a random phenomenon or corruption, the genus of same-sex erotic attraction is a vital, important and indispensable component of creation, overall, and human development, in particular. In human society, it is a "seven percent solution," an element built in as an intercession, so to speak, into the species' merely procreative impulse grounded in male dominion over women, children and territory.

Those experiencing primarily same-sex erotic attraction are motivated by something other than the procreative-territorial impulse, and harbor not only a passion for those of their own sex, but also for the disenfranchised victims of male-dominated society, including women, children and, as no longer useful to the perpetuation of male control, the elderly and infirm. The history of human social development is characterized by two currents in conflict.

The first is grounded in the male-dominated nuclear family and its extension, in which the male rules the roost, dominating women in the exercise of his reproductive power, and his offspring for purposes of extending his "franchise," so to speak. Boys are raised to be warriors to fight his territorial resource-capture wars or to become corporate clones in the administration of the franchise. Girls are raised to reproduce and care for more offspring in their early years. In this paradigm, the elderly and infirm are cast off, generally, as useless.

Males clash with other males in this "family values" paradigm to compete for territory or resources, or form expedient alliances to gain more collective control and fend off challengers. These form into tribes or nations in which the king male, the most brutish and gains ascendancy stays in power to rule over an extended dominion through the perpetuation of his family line, also known as hereditary succession. While queens are allowed periodically to protect the integrity of the overall process, in general women remain docile second-class citizens, children duly subservient, and populations captured through conquest enslaved to perform rote labor. Subject peoples are kept in line through ignorance, religious superstition and, of course, downright repression.

The second current is, in a word, egalitarian. It rejects the dynamics of the "family values" model, asserting that women, children and subject peoples retain as much right to enfranchisement as dominant males. It intercedes to fight on behalf of the subject peoples and is an alliance of defiant women, rebellious slaves and subject peoples, inspired by concepts of democratic, just government and determined to dash the crippling influence of religious superstition through general education to advance scientific knowledge and the power of reason in each and every individual.

There is no middle ground between these two currents, even though history is filled with futile efforts at trying for it. We know where the first current comes from: nature's mandate for self-preservation through reproduction. But where does the second current come from?

It comes from a push-back by all or part of those repressed in the first current. But it is more than push-back. It is inspired by concepts of universal harmony, beauty and visions for a free, happy and creative life for all, and they come from persons not captured in the motive dynamics of the "family values" currently. That defines us, ladies and gentlemen, us. It is where we gays come in.

While nature operates by its powerful, overriding demand for its reproduction, it also provides for the mitigating effects of that through an equally-powerful expression of erotic passion directed to the same sex, though limited to a small fraction of the total population.

From the earliest human records, egalitarian anti-tyrannical teachings have come from our words and pens, from Socrates and Plato to the psalms and benevolence of King David, through pro-republican leaders of the Italian renaissance to Shakespeare, and the myriad of our gay sisters and brothers whose lives have gone unrecorded who have populated human history.

Our identity in the long sweep of humanity finds our natural same-sex erotic attraction and fight for egalitarian and democratic values coexisting and inseparable. I call this overall disposition our "gay sensibility." It accounts for why we are hated by the powerful "alpha males" of the "family values" paradigm. At the heart of the matter, we are their arch enemies who have created the political and other institutions to liberate their enslaved women, children and subjects. The American Revolution represents a truly radical, history-changing triumph of the egalitarian current against the "family values" one.

COMMON SENSE

THE IDEAS THAT BURNED IN THE hearts of a people inspired to fight for their independence from a brutal "family values" monarchy, on behalf of sustainable institutions of a democratic republic, came from visionaries like Thomas Paine, whose pamphlet, *Common Sense* (1776), railed against the very idea of monarchy and hereditary succession on behalf of a universal vision of a stable egalitarian alternative. It can't be overstated how amazingly radical the core tenant underlying the American revolution actually was in its time. The most important assumption associated with the male-dominated nuclear family was pronounced invalid as a premise for the governance of humankind's affairs. An unprecedented rejection of the notion of a monarch ruling through hereditary succession was at the very heart of what the revolution stood for.

In *Common Sense*, inflaming growing anger in the colonies against British rule at exactly the right moment, made this Paine's most emphatic point. Mankind's affairs, he insisted, must not be governed by a monarch whose hereditary perpetuation inevitably generates offspring of inferior moral and intellectual powers to rule after him. To Paine, it was not some particularly egregious tax or other policy that was cause for grievance, but the notion of monarchy, itself. Paine's view was far more radical than many other U.S. Founding Fathers, who saw redressing oppressive policies as the primary cause for revolt but who were otherwise content to allow the monarchy to continue. Paine and his allies were more universally visionary, harkening to a day when all people, regardless of color, gender or current social status, would be free and equal, able to choose their governmental representatives based on their merits and to develop and realize their full talents and potential. Tenuous as they remain, such notions are taken for granted today, even as we strive to extend them to the one remaining class of persons in this country still denied them – us. But they were hardly commonly held values on the eve of the American revolution.

It can be credibly argued that gay sensibility – an alternate sensual perspective inherent in our portion of humanity naturally erotically inclined toward the same sex – was an indispensable component in the overthrow of the very notion of monarchy. After all, even if virtually invisible, there were proportionately as many of us around then as now. Straight men adhering to the privileges of their dominion over women and children were naturally loath to call for the overthrow of the very system that had given them their advantage for eons. To them, monarchy was a lawful extension of their own vaunted male supremacy. Those not centered on species reproduction and attendant nuclear families and territorial control would more likely consider a fundamentally alternative way of ordering mankind's affairs.

Thus, it was Plato, author of *The Republic* (380 BC) and others of our tribe, who developed the earliest cogent concepts of how a republic, not tyranny, best serves humanity's interest. Gays, aligned with free-minded women, children, slaves and others abused by tyranny, were best inclined to push for more than petty reforms, but for a revolution against the monarchical system, itself. There is no evidence that Thomas Paine was gay. He left his wife in England early in his life and never remarried through his exploits sparking both the American revolution and French revolutions. He assailed not only monarchy, but the institutional church that controlled people's minds with religious superstition (*The Age of Reason*, 1795). Eventually too radical for almost everyone (Thomas Jefferson remained one of his few friends), only eight people attended his funeral.

But there is evidence that Paine's revolutionary colleague Alexander Hamilton was gay. Hamilton and his Federalist allies recognized the potential and importance in a wedding of reason rejecting superstition, anti-monarchical democratic values and organization, and the strength of a union of all the colonies. Many letters, veritable love letters, from Hamilton to fellow radical abolitionist Col. John Laurens (1754-1782) exist. Laurens and Hamilton were both aides de camp under General Washington. The beloved Laurens represented an interesting link between Hamilton and Paine. It was the same Laurens who paired up with Paine on a trip to France in 1781 to raise money for the American cause.

Simply pronouncing Hamilton "gay" doesn't work, however. It's complicated, given his heterosexual affairs and many children. But for same-sex attracted persons to live complicated lives was common in those times. For example, contemporary gays may find it hard to believe that same-sex attracted people did not commonly engage in sexual intercourse back then.

But, notwithstanding different times, coping mechanisms and ranges of allowed behaviors through the ages, it is safe to say that feelings of same-sex erotic arousal, ranging in intensity and mood from the "bathwater drinking" passion to more subtle varieties, has always been the same.

Not counting cases of rape, coercion, prostitution, impersonal bathhouse or t-room varieties of sex or orgies – constituting the bulk of historical records of same-sex encounters – intimate, affectionate and reciprocal erotic dimensions to sustained same-sex relationships are basically of three types, and always have been. The first is when one of the parties is erotically attracted to the other, and the relationship is intimate and emotionally reciprocal even through the other party does not share the same kind of erotic attraction and may be, in fact, straight. The straight party may or may not be aware of the friend's erotic feelings. This kind of relationship makes up the vast majority of intimate same-sex relationships where erotic attraction is a factor. The second is when there is erotic reciprocity, far more common now than ever before, that is consummated by sexual intercourse. The third is when there is erotic reciprocity, but without a context, for any number of reasons, that permits sexual fulfillment or public expressions of affection.

All three types are legitimate and widespread, and are not circumscribed by age difference, masculine or feminine characteristics or any other factors. One or both of the parties in each of the cases often seeks to attain high degrees of exclusivity for the relationship. In addition, there is a fourth form of same-sex reciprocal relationship involving persons, one or both, with same-sex erotic passions, but which are not factors in the relationship. These are non-sexual friendships that are keenly enhanced by one or both of the parties' special capacity for same-sex empathy that introduces levels of care and consideration surpassing the garden variety usually-superficial and condition-related friendships among straights. This fourth form is also very common, resulting in some of the most sustained same-sex friendships over lifetimes. It includes what can happen when the erotic passions at play in the other three options fade. It can also apply as gay empathy, or "simpatico," finds affection for genuine spirits regardless of gender or sexual orientation, and among "posses," cliques or circles of gay friends. Heightened empathy usually makes gays – those not jaded or ground down by their own cynicism – very good employers and collaborators in the workplace. It is a quality that has a strong aversion to cruelty and injustice.

How Hamilton best fits or rides along this spectrum of same-sex erotic and affectionate passions, such was how he was gay. Likewise for Abraham Lincoln, who like Hamilton, married and had children. Lincoln had a same-sex relationship with Joshua Fry Speed, with whom he shared a bed for four years, 1837 to 1841 (long before becoming president). As Hamilton wrote love letters to

Laurens, Lincoln wrote them to Speed, saying "You know my desire to befriend you is everlasting." Lincoln biographer Carl Sandburg declared each had "a streak of lavender and spots as soft as May violets" for the other. As Hamilton in his Federalist Papers, Lincoln took up the cause to "preserve the union" in the Civil War. As Hamilton was fiercely anti-slavery, Lincoln became the "Great Emancipator" by signing the Emancipation Proclamation. Both men were passionate same-sex lovers, and champions to the death of sustainable justice and democracy. To the death, indeed. Both died prematurely from gun shots wounds inflicted by enemies.

STONEWALL AMID ANTI-WAR FERMENT

THERE'S NO COINCIDENCE THAT THE MODERN gay liberation movement, that which associates its founding with the riots at the Stonewall Inn in New York's Greenwich Village in late June 1969, arose in the context of the civil rights movement for racial equality and the growing anti-Vietnam War movement. Post-modernist historians diminish the importance of this confluence by suggesting that, at best, the gay liberation explosion took the other social movements as a model, or occasion, for its own. However, they were intrinsically interconnected, and it is in that interconnection that a crucial component of what it means to be gay is found.

There was a remarkable correspondence of events the weekend of the Stonewall Riots that underscores this point. Common wisdom is that the riots, which broke out as the Stonewall Inn was closing at 3 a.m. in the warm summer early morning hours of Saturday, June 28, 1969 were in part sparked by the mourning of thousands of gays on occasion of the funeral of gay icon Judy Garland the afternoon before.

Garland, born in Minnesota as Frances Ethel Gumm, was only 47 when she died in London of an accidental drug overdose on June 22, 1969. The young teen star of *The Wizard of Oz*, she struggled in her adult life, marrying four times, and took comfort from gay male friends, often hanging out in gay clubs, as she bravely undertook comebacks in her career. Her body flown to New York on Thursday, June 26, more than 20,000 paid their respects at a funeral home that day, an overwhelming number of them gay. On Friday, a closed funeral was held, while thousands held vigil outside. That night, in the wee hours of Saturday, street people lingering outside the Stonewall Inn (not the patrons inside) clashed with police in what sparked a running battle over a number of days.

But something else happened at the same time which, it can be credibly argued, was even more acutely associated with that memorable weekend. It was the publication of the June 27, 1969 edition of *Life* magazine, which did a first for its time of dedicating its cover and 12 pages inside to a high-school yearbook portraits-style format of 242 photographs of mostly 18-to-20 year old rosy-cheeked boys who had been killed in just one week, May 28 to June 3, in Vietnam. The feature included one such face on the cover and the blaring headline, "The Faces of the American Dead: One Week's Toll." Life's plans for the issue received considerable notoriety prior to its publication, and urging from the U.S. military not to do it. Historians of the anti-Vietnam War movement called it "a significant factor in reducing pro-war sentiment."

As a young gay man on the West Coast who had come out two months earlier by way of my first significant gay encounter, I was unaware of the Stonewall Riots but was mesmerized by that issue of *Life*. I had just graduated, with honors, with a Masters from the Pacific School of Religion in Berkeley, and in my three years there had seen a lot of demonstrations, riots, National Guard troops and tear gas as the anti-war movement grew. I was anti-war, myself, though it was the civil rights movement, and the assassinations of Martin Luther King, Jr. and Bobby Kennedy in the spring of 1968, that really catalyzed my personal transformation from a small-town boy who completed college on a baseball scholarship into an impassioned political being. My coming out was facilitated not by post-Stonewall ferment, but by a conference I attended the previous fall of the Council on Religion and the Homosexual, an outgrowth of the struggles of the earlier gay rights efforts of the Mattachine Society.

My actual coming out on April 24, 1969, and my first intimate encounter then, helped, I believe, to open my physical and emotional sensibilities to respond viscerally to the unspeakable horror of what the June 27 Life magazine depicted. Unlike today's volunteer armies, most drafted to die in Vietnam were just teenagers. My younger brother was in Vietnam on a boat that launched swift boats in the Mekong Delta. I'd already learned that two of my friends had died there, including one who had one of the most amazing personalities, with the good looks to accompany it, I'd ever known. Hispanic, he was just a kid, and had no way to avoid the draft. My affirmation of my homosexuality became inseparably connected to the empathy I felt for the thousands of boys dying senselessly in Vietnam. This is the point that Christopher Isherwood suggested in what I wrote last week; that we, as homosexuals, play a special role in society by virtue of our propensity for loving our own sex, to resist the savage carnage of war and its brutal disregard for the real human beings suffering it. Not merely a collateral, it is an indispensable part of our gay identity, of who we are.

PEACEMAKERS

> "There is no such thing as a good war, or a
> bad peace"
>   —Benjamin Franklin

THE STUNNING CONFLUENCE OF EVENTS THAT occurred on the weekend of June 27, 1969 – *Life*'s magazine's extraordinary edition lining up 12 pages of high school yearbook-style photographs of one week's worth of deaths of young American soldiers in Vietnam hitting newsstands the same weekend as the Stonewall Riots in New York's Greenwich Village – is an amazingly poignant, fitting historical testimonial to the symbiotic nature of the civil rights, feminist, anti-war and gay liberation movements. That the modern gay liberation movement, which later adopted the Stonewall Riots as its point of departure, occurred to the day as one of the strongest national statements against the Vietnam War began confronting the national consciousness, provides a telling and decisive clue: Our gay liberation movement was not born in isolation.

It was part and parcel of a social upheaval which had universal justice and equality as its object. What made the

Vietnam War so bad was its sheer lack of credible national purpose. On the contrary, it brought home the warning by President Eisenhower a few years earlier about the danger of a "military industrial complex" running the nation to its own ends.

A general in World War II, Eisenhower knew the abject horror of war, and vowed never to permit America to go to war during his two terms as president. When inaugurated in 1952, America had kicked off another war in Korea, and Eisenhower ended it as soon after being sworn in as he could. But the escalation toward war in Vietnam in the 1960s had the benefit of no such countervailing resolve. Given the mainstream American resistance to the civil rights and War on Poverty struggles of the 1960s, the assassinations of Martin Luther King, Jr., and Robert Kennedy in 1968 led to an angry surge of opposition to tens of thousands of our nation's young being drafted to die in the jungles of a pointless war.

I was in that surge. It included an imperative to cast off all the trappings of social oppression that the captains of the "military and industrial complex" used to hold us down. Coming out, and the launch of the modern gay movement, was part and parcel of a far wider social convulsion that was happening. Thus I, after co-founding the Berkeley Gay Liberation Front, wrote the *Gay Sunshine* newspaper's first editorial entitled, "Who Needs It?," saying the movement should "represent all those who understand themselves as oppressed – politically oppressed by an oppressor that not only is down on homosexuality, but equally down on all things that are not white, straight, middle class, pro-establishment...It should harken to a greater cause – the cause of human liberation, of which homosexual liberation is just one aspect."

I was then chosen to be the first-ever "official" gay liberation spokesman invited to address a major anti-war rally in San Francisco's Golden Gate Park. All this was entirely in keeping with the kind of fervor and wider social justice purposefulness that ignited the Stonewall movement. We gays, after all, hated the war because we were especially inclined to feel empathetic, same-sex attraction to many of those young men being slaughtered. Dads cheered them on. Moms couldn't defy their husbands. So it was up to us to really spearhead the anti-war movement, and we did.

DIVIDE AND CONQUER

BUT NONE OF THIS HAPPENED UNCONTESTED, and the counter-punch came with a vengeance, though in a form that caught most unaware. While the strident, militaristic right wing required our focus, an insidious and toxic counter-insurgent influence infiltrated the anti-war ferment from within: the "sex, drugs and rock-and-roll counterculture." I documented earlier the covert, pro-fascist intelligence elements behind this.

It was a noxious mix of radical hedonism and post-modernist social dissembling. I was a first-hand witness. The social disintegration aspect involved socio-political ideologies that rejected the bonds of social justice-inspired solidarity linking the anti-war, civil rights, feminist and gay movements. In the postmodernism of the despicable Michel Foucault and his ilk, it is each against all: no one is trusted and all authority, even scientific authority, is to be questioned, disregarded and resisted.

Therefore, the social justice bonds I wrote about in my *Gay Sunshine* editorial came under fire: to them, the gay movement was about gays, and that was it. Talk about "divide and conquer," it was the oldest counter-insurgency trick in the book! It worked. Moreover, with radical anarcho-hedonism replacing social consciousness with the personal pursuit of pleasure, post-modernist imperatives demanded a rejection of all restraint. The gay movement devolved quickly into the urban anarcho-hedonist excesses of the 1970s, bearing trappings of sexual addiction and habitual fads, creating the incubator from which AIDS arose.

Social activism thus "taken out," the nation crept back toward war. With Reagan came indifference to gays in crisis, non-democratic precedents to fighting wars, and greed-laden spread of domestic debt slavery. What happened to America in the quarter-century between 1963, when the national ethos was defined by Martin Luther King, Jr.'s "I Have a Dream" speech, and 1987, when it became defined by the "Greed is Good" speech by Gordon Gekko in the movie, *Wall Street*? Stemming today's perilous careen toward the "might makes right" radical "social Darwinist" tenants of the Ryan budget, now embraced by an entire political party, requires a hard look at how the shift in that 1963-1987 period happened. June 1969 was pivotal. I've written about the confluence of events then that involved, on the one hand, a major ratcheting up of the anti-Vietnam War movement and, on the other, the "big bang" birth of the modern gay liberation movement around the Stonewall riots.

Those two simultaneous factors were the product of one of the most moral and courageous periods in history. Building on earlier achievements of the civil rights movement for racial equality, the U.S. population rose up to, for the first time in the nation's history, actually stop a war. Led by morally-inspired youth who risked all – jobs, careers, family ties, friends and personal safety – Americans shook the very foundations of traditional power in the U.S. They threatened to bring down that "military and industrial complex" governed by white men, all who felt enfranchised to systematically degrade the role of women, racial minorities and workers, to hate homosexuality, and to order tens of thousands of teenagers to ugly deaths in the jungles of Vietnam.

Such was what we called "The Man," and "The Man" was being seriously shaken by a turbulent sea of righteous anger flooding the streets of his cities, surging like a terrible harbinger of Judgment Day against his cruel injustice. So came our gay liberation movement. Inspired by the courage around us, legions of our own tribe, risking even more by "coming out" than the rest, stood up and, bursting with our own courage, claimed our right, the right of us all, to full integrity and our rightful, unique role in the progress of humankind. Overall, it was the most amazing period since the Revolution in American history, spawning and empowered by, both, our gay liberation movement. It was the full force of the "I Have a Dream" speech played out on the streets of America.

But it didn't last. As the war began subsiding, there was a rot spreading within the popular uprising whose effect was to turn people away from a fiery demand for justice for all and instead have them curl inward in pursuit of self-centered hedonistic excess. The influence had been there all along. But as the fervor of the movement waned, it began to assert itself and take over, the flip side of the pursuit of justice and happiness for all. It involved a shift to a preoccupation with selfish desires over the well-being of the overall community. Spurring this tendency had a long history.

Since the rise of industrialism in the 18th century, captains of industry and privilege sought to devise ways to undermine the capacity to resist among those they sought to exploit. They saw collective resistance as the biggest roadblock to their unfettered success, and specifically, they were determined to prevent anything like the American revolution from ever happening again.

Philosophies of the individual were developed and propagated, from Max Stirner's *The Ego and Its Own*, to the theories of Friedrich Nietzsche and Sigmund Freud, and others, about empowering selfish self-obsession against social conscience. The science of "sexology" was devised as one variant.

The approach was formed out of a corruption of Charles Darwin's theory of natural selection, the notion that self-centered humans are by nature driven by two impulses, one toward socially responsible behavior and the other in selfish rebellion against it. The tension was defined in terms of sexual urges. In typology drawn from Greek mythology, these contending urges were seen as Apollonian (socially responsible) versus Dionysian (pleasure seeking).

Key to this theory was its denial and suppression of a third natural human impulse toward advancing the general good of humankind and associated with the Greek myth of Prometheus.

Fast forwarding to the 1960s, the deliberate cultivation and mainstreaming of a Dionysian "sex, drugs and rock and roll" counterculture was unleashed on the social ferment of that era to defuse it. That counterculture lured people to abandon social justice on behalf of individual radical hedonism, to "turn on, tune in and drop out." The mantra to "drop out," to abandon the pursuit of one's creative potential in an effort to shape a better world – namely, to extinguish the Promethean impulse – was its most insidious component. A massive offensive, it worked.

The events surrounding and subsequent to the modern gay movement-founding Stonewall Riots of June 1969 are relevant to our cause today. It's not just ancient history. First was the spectacular context that gave rise to the modern movement, a by-product of the greatest surge of popular passion for civil rights, justice and an end to a senseless war in the history of the U.S.

Second was the rapid devolution of that idealism and activism into an excessively self-centered urban anarcho-hedonism in the early 1970s creating the preconditions for the AIDS crisis and, most tragically, involving an abandonment by hundreds of thousands of gays of their creative work.

The creative energy that powered the first-ever successful effort by the people to actually stop a war was, by the socially-engineered "tune in, turn on, drop out" so-called "counterculture," deflated into a selfish, habitual obsession with sensual delights that involved dropping the pursuit of creative work. In the San Francisco gay ghetto, the social pressure was to quit work and go on welfare, as "Castro clones" spent days on street corners in conformist lumberjack dress and nights at the baths. This was how it went down for Ken Horne, the first known person to die from AIDS. He'd come to San Francisco seeking a career in ballet, but got caught in the "scene," soon abandoning his dream to take a menial job so he could maximize his time cruising for sex.

I felt the pressure acutely, as my gay liberation colleagues pressured me to quit my job as a reporter for the *Berkeley Barb* and go on "aid to the totally dependent." I didn't.

Previously marginalized institutions of increasingly graphic pornography, seamy bars, disco clubs, bathhouses, S and M torture chambers, and countless opportunities for anonymous, impersonal sex came to define the gay culture and lifestyle.

Later, gradually recovering from the AIDS horror and the loss of 400,000 beautiful human lives between and 1981-1996, our gay culture suffered an acute post-traumatic stress syndrome of denial and conformist and nonconformist extremism. (Typically, writing his "coming out" book, *The Confession*, in 2006, former New Jersey governor James McGreevey talked about life in the closet as a "divided self," but made no mention of AIDS even as it was obviously swirling all around him during his many dangerous forays into anonymous sex.) But the 2011 highly-acclaimed revival of *The Normal Heart*, Larry Kramer's gripping 1984 play about the horrible early days of AIDS, signaled a shift. A smash on Broadway, winning Tony Awards and being made into a movie in 2014, it was the first really hard look at AIDS that our wider community has been willing to face up to since the whole thing broke out. A new opportunity exists to revisit the assumptions of our current gay culture, especially the components carried forward from the pre-AIDS culture of the 1970s.

While no one is advocating a repudiation of all erotic features of our culture, the move toward institutionalizing stable and loyal gay relationships through marriage is a positive impulse toward something more substantial and humanizing. On the other hand, "queer theory" advocates an escalation of non-conformity, pursuing ever more exotic and bizarre pursuits of perceived pleasure and anti-authoritarianism, trying to establish these as authentic for the future of our culture. But the debate about gay culture as "assimilationist versus anti-assimilationist" is wrong on both sides.

In the courageous struggle for full equality, gay marriage is now the cutting edge. But the issue is one of full equality, not whether or not marriage is the right thing for everybody. Who wants to merely assimilate into our present militaristic and testosterone-saturated culture? Marriage doesn't imply assimilation as long as we stay true to our gay nature, which to the core is resistant to the cruel and dehumanizing currents of the dominant culture. The defining characteristics of gay identity – gay sensibility, an alternate sensual perspective and constructive non-conformity – form the basis of the transformative role our tribe is assigned to play in the evolution of our wider culture. Our job is to engage and transform society, as we always have.

Wars will never save humanity. Humanity will prosper and advance in peace only by the work that we gays and our allies do. Our own salvation is in our creativity and our work, too. Tennessee Williams knew this. As hard as he partied at night, he was always in his studio to write for hours every morning. His work was his life, it was the core of his gay identity.

Gay culture in the future shall be built around creativity and the unique contributions we bring to forging a better world.

Few can disagree that modern American popular culture has drifted toward increased demands for and obsession with youth, physique and instant gratification. This trend owes to the tectonic shift underlying the rise of the Madison Avenue-based marketing industry that has moved American self-perception from producer to consumer. Our culture now tells us we, as a democratic nation, are composed not so much of citizens who share in the responsibility for the best interests of our population as a whole, but of consumers. We're no longer knowledge-hungry, discerning, inventive people who build and fix things, but we're inhaling, insatiable repositories of earthly delights.

This shift was facilitated by the introduction of credit cards on a wide scale in the 1960s. People were told they could have whatever they wanted, like big-eyed kids in a candy store. This shifted the population from goal-directed resource marshaling to debt-strangling accumulation of toys and "conveniences." Now, from student loans to mortgages and credit card debt, millions have become bound by "debt slavery." Fresh out of college and to the grave, lives (like nations) are dictated by the imperative to pay debts to the banks, pressured to cast aside dreams and ambitions of creative work in favor of whatever menial job is available. Under "debt slavery," mediocrity is the order of the day, and explains why the U.S. is falling behind other nations in science, education and invention.

Our gay tribe is caught in this bind, but often with far worse consequences because many among us lack the same kind of social networks to see us through tough times. While the lure of hedonistic pleasures permeates all of society, the social bonds of family and friends are more likely to mitigate such impacts on the destiny of a wayward soul. But in gay culture, there is a contrary tendency of fair-weather "friends" to encourage a descent down that path without regard for the consequences.

In the wider culture, as youth and looks fade, families – including spouses, children and in-laws – provide enduring comfort and meaning in the transition from hedonistic pleasure-seeking.

But in gay culture, such alternative options often aren't there. Too many gay people become depressed by the prospect of age and a loss of looks even before such conditions are present.

Rather than cultivating one's capacity to engineer a meaningful life, the passive consumer of earthly delights bemoans his or her fate as a crumbling, fading violet, pumping even more iron in the gym to fend off the inevitable, seeking even more impersonal trysts to prove at least a temporary worth in the world of hedonism for its own sake, and sinking into despair over an inability to maintain a supposedly desirable figure.

All the while, those so obsessed hate what they are unable to prevent from becoming, themselves, by lashing out at those already there, denigrating all those they perceive less attractive than themselves. It isn't just young gays who commit suicide for being tormented by bullies. It's older gays, too, of all ages, tormented by the sense of emptiness and uselessness in a candy store where only the prettiest cookies have value. "Who says 'It Gets Better?,'" one astute gay friend observed rhetorically. For gays, unless there are lots of financial security and social bonds, it too often doesn't, or not for long, anyway.

Valuing sex and sexual partners as acts and objects of consumption, as encouraged in our whole culture, makes matters worse for gays. There is an emotional short-circuit associated with repeated, habitual impersonal sex that leaves lasting scars. It can become very difficult, nearly impossible, to simply drop impersonal sex and pick up a meaningful relationship (that isn't "open"). It is a special tragedy for so many gay people to fall into such depersonalized patterns, because if anything, we are created as people-centered creatures, inclined more than most to lift up those who are in need by the strength of loving empathy and empower them. The worst fate for a gay person – the one that takes him or her the farthest from the root of a gay soul – is to become jaded, to become indifferent and cruel. It is a product of our wider culture, for sure, but there is little in our gay culture to insulate us from it, or to cure us from it.

The 1960s so-called "counterculture" and the mores of post-modernism, as preached by Michel Foucault and others, promoted a form of radical consumerism, including the consumption of people as mere sex objects, in the name of the sexual revolution and rejection of authority. As such, sexual acts of the post-modern rebel were touted more as acts of defiance against power than anything like love or romance. Regrettably, gay culture fell victim to this madness 40 years ago and has yet to cast it off. If anything, gays should be leading the nation's way back to being a productive, creative, caring people.

Regarding the consequences of the national cultural shift since the 1970s away from productive and generous notions of the individual to selfish self-interested ones is the 2010 powerful film documentary *Regeneration*, narrated and co-produced by actor Ryan Gosling, available On-Demand and iTunes. *Regeneration* tells about the systematic institutional and media-engineered creation of the "Me" generation that has, as a result, effectively "tuned out" wider social realities in favor of self-centered consumerism. This has led to unprecedented encroachments on democratic institutions (such as the U.S. Supreme Court's "Citizens United" decision allowing unlimited and anonymous corporate and individual campaign contributions), a steep decline in the nation's competitiveness intellectually, and an "empathy gap," the level of apathy and cynicism about prospects for real change that threaten the nation's most core values.

IT DOES NOT BEND ON ITS OWN

DR. MARTIN LUTHER KING, JR. SAID, "The arc of the moral universe is long but it bends toward justice," but he added, "It does not bend on its own. It bends because each of us in our own ways put our hand on that arc and bend it in the direction of justice." Remove those hands, abandon what Abraham Lincoln called the "better angels of our nature," in favor of unbridled personal and corporate greed and cultural side effects, such as society's implicit sanctioning of rude and hateful behavior, yelling and honking in traffic, insulting persons without remorse, include, as I pointed out last time, the depersonalization of humans as ravished objects of consumption, as "meat," or not. In this context, increasingly hollow, bought-and-paid-for democratic institutions are allowing the greatest disparity in the distribution of wealth in the nation's history, as all the while the entire world sinks into a prolonged economic malaise, a potential new great global depression savaged by rampant poverty, war and disease.

The daunting task of reversing these trends confronts everybody, and the gay community in particular because of our considerable talent at orchestrating such reversals shown through history. Faced with this burden, a puzzling title appeared proclaiming, *Victory: The Triumphant Gay Revolution* (2012). Victory? Written by attorney Linda Hirshman, her first work on LGBT matters, the book's title suggests that, well, we've won. What's to worry about now? Are we to forget that we are in the grips of one of the roughest presidential campaigns in U.S. history, the first with the prospects of billions of anonymous campaign contributions thanks to "Citizens United?" Are we to forget that President Obama has instituted more strides toward full equality and respect for the LGBT community, more by light years, than any other president in history? Are we to forget that political opponents have promised to reverse and repeal all of the advances that Obama instituted? And under Trump, they tried. Victory already? Really?

One wonders if this notion could deter the kind of extraordinary political mobilization the gay community is being called to, with all that we've gained and hope to gain on the line. The book by this avowedly heterosexual author panders to the gay community and has a decidedly pro-Republican slant. Notwithstanding considerable shortcomings in its history (the complete absence of reference to Randy Shilts' devastating journalistic work about AIDS, *And the Band Played On*, being one example), it diminishes Obama's role (saying at one point he "insults and ignores the gay community") and elevates those of Republicans like the attorney for the gay Log Cabin Republicans by saying, "He finds his advocacy perfectly consistent with his conservative principle that every man should be treated strictly on his own merit."

The book culminates its cited "march to victory" with the work of super-rich moguls, showing how Republican-led pro-gay organizations threw their weight around in recent elections. "Victory" in this sense implies handing off the movement to the one percent of one percent of the super-rich, who don't care what people do in their bedrooms (for now) as long as they hand over their cash to defeating Democrats. It hints to the secretive "Political OUTgiving Conference" held in May 15-16, 2010 in Chicago that Lou Chibbaro reported in the May 27, 2010 *Washington Blade* entitled, "Rare Peek Behind Closed Doors of Secret Gay Donor Confab." Key organizers of the conference were Patrick Guerriero, former president of the Log Cabin Republicans, and Bill Smith, former aide to Karl Rove.

Former Bush Chief of Staff Rove headed the largest post-"Citizens United" so-called "Super-PAC," American Crossroads, and invented the new strategy of gathering monied interests in secret conferences to raise the unlimited amounts they're now allowed to give.

THE ROLE OF EMPATHY

THE CORE THESIS OF THIS BOOK is the novel notion that same-sex erotic attraction is a variant and derivative of the natural bond between humans more akin to empathy than the physically reproductive impulse.

It is designed to set a framework for further scientific pursuit of this idea based on its importance in the following ways: (1) It liberates the homosexual impulse from being understood as a form of deviation or corruption of the heterosexual reproductive impulse. If that is how it is seen, even if it is seen as a consequence of natural processes, then it must be that the impulse is somehow inferior to an ideal norm, which is species reproduction. The political response in this construct is to see it either as a danger or benign for society — either it must be repressed, or can be tolerated as non-harmful. (2) It links and interconnects the homosexual impulse with other attributes associated with empathy, including its impulse to serve others through natural healing-like gifts, such as for the creative arts, and an affinity for the underdog, such as women, children and the elderly and dispossessed in the face of societal leadership that brutalizes them.

What we call empathy, science is learning, is a critically important attribute supplied by nature for the success of species, as I have shown earlier. Linked to notions of altruism and the sacrifice of the individual for the benefit of the species, it marks the difference between survival and failure in many circumstances observed in nature. Therefore, for humanity, it is an indispensable and positive element of culture. That's where we homosexuals fit.

The dominant society has defined false parameters, internalized by homosexuals, for the very definition and expectations of same-sex erotic attraction, linking it unduly to simply sexual contexts, including extreme and bizarre forms, and, overall, consigning the phenomenon to evidences of weakness and inferiority. But this is based on a false epistemology derived from the very brutal nature of straight male dominated militaristic culture, itself. Straight male dominion and its savage might-makes-right axioms justifying the subjugation of women, children and subordinate labor, including slaves and conquered people, to the tyrant's lust for accumulating and preserving the natural and human resources needed to enhance that dominion, suffered its first major setback in modern times in the radical Enlightenment ferment of the 1700s that resulted in the American revolution.

The core political notion underlying the American revolution was that human beings are valued according to their merits as contributors to the social good, and not simply because they are straight males or straight male heirs of royalty and privilege. The straight-male premise of monarchy, thus, was violently opposed to this American revolution, and devoted the next century to undoing its impact while also conniving ways to ensure it would never happen again. On the latter point, it encouraged continental philosophies that argued for the primacy of the isolated individual ego in all arenas of human behavior, undermining and discrediting in the process, notions of human empathy and solidarity as primary.

To the extent they created a philosophical movement to this end, it produced (and promoted) individuals like Nietzsche and Freud, who took the isolated ego and bifurcated it into two parts, the socialized ego and the animalistic, anti-social id. In Nietzsche's *Gay Science*, the title of a book which is actually about about poetry, the ego is identified with the Greek god Apollo, and the id with Dionysus, the rebellious lover of pleasure for its own sake. Same-sex erotic impulse was brought under this false construct as a manifestation of Dionysus, and that core notion has persisted to this day.

However, as I am right, according to the preponderance of evidence I have accumulated in these pages, then the same-sex erotic impulse is more accurately associated with the Greek god of Prometheus, the god who acted in defiance of Zeus but on behalf of humanity.

The Promethean archetype was at the heart of the revolutionary ferment of the latter 18th century, both in Europe and the American colonies. It represented exactly what the straight-male dominated old monarchies hated and sought to extinguish. The rise of the modern gay liberation movement since the Stonewall riots in 1969 provided the opportunity for a massive outpouring of the Promethean spirit across the land. Prometheus had been willing to suffer for his disobedience because he had given life to humanity and he, too, was ultimately liberated.

However, the enemies of the life-giving Promethean spirit that had created American democracy and helped to spread it around the world pounced on the ferment of the late 1960s with a new, escalated round of self-centered hedonistic extremism that diverted the gay movement, and society as a whole, toward the "me" generation of mindless consumerism.

7

Gay Science

I BEGAN THE SERIES OF COLUMNS THAT has resulted in this book in October 2010 with three chapters entitled the same as this, and as I prepare to conclude, I'll reiterate why I began that way. First, the title, "Gay Science," has a double meaning.

In the first case, it refers to my case against 19th century German philosopher Friedrich Nietzsche, as in his book *Gay Science* who proclaimed among other things the "death of God." My "Gay Science," is contrasted to the flawed Nietzschean anarchistic "will to power" concept that contributed to the rise of Nazism and in late 1960s to the radical anarcho-hedonist shift in American culture. That shift was away from humanist values associated with Eleanor Roosevelt's post-World War II "International Declaration of Human Rights" to our current consumerist, selfish self-interest defined culture.

In the second, my "Gay Science" refers to the role of same-sex erotic attraction as a core component in nature, a derivative of the essential dissymmetry of the universe, itself, and among organized life forms, in the indispensable role for heightened empathetic and altruistic impulses behaviors in successful societies. As much, it is contrary to neo-Darwinian "survival of the fittest" and "social Darwinist" theories. I contend that same-sex erotic attraction, although manifested as strongly sexual, actually derives from empathetic and altruistic components of natural behavior, and not as a deviation of the reproductive impulse.

These two meanings of "Gay Science" combined, I've written about the collision of a newly socially-affirmed natural role for same-sex erotic attraction with its context, namely, the last 40 years' cultural paradigm shift. In so doing, I've challenged, among other things, the prevalent view that the modern post-Stonewall gay liberation movement is a cutting edge of that cultural shift toward selfish hedonism. To the contrary, it was swept into adopting the crazed urban-centered sexual addictive behaviors of the 1970s that led to the AIDS epidemic.

While urban homosexuals have yet to consciously shed such effects and residual patterns remain, positive signs exist, including the push for gay marriage and a better respect for the cultivation of talents manifesting our natural "constructive non-conformity" that benefit society overall. This series and this book have sought to contribute to a new dialogue on these lines, toward what gay playwright Tony Kushner, in an introduction to a published script of Larry Kramer's *The Normal Heart,* called the need for a "a new gay morality" better reflecting our true nature and purpose.

It is forward-directed, recognizing that many committed to the current gay culture may find it foreign or off-putting. Old terms like "sex-negative" or "self-loathing," born in a bygone era to defame anyone who did not affirm anarcho-hedonistic sexual excess, do not apply here.

As a San Francisco-area pioneer of the modern gay movement, I lived through it all. Overwhelmed by the hedonistic excess of the 1970s, I stepped aside to a self-imposed exile. I survived all that ensued somehow and have since felt compelled to understand what happened and share my insights honestly. Thus, my *Gay Science.*

Little did I realize then – as my 1970s effort was failing to lead the movement toward more universal and compassionate civil rights purposes, free from the maelstrom of depersonalizing radical hedonism – that my colleagues and I had a singular adversary dedicated to fueling that maelstrom's power nearby. Gay postmodern philosopher Michel Foucault, whose acquired stature was the creation of some foul and malicious social engineering effort I have no doubt, was lecturing in the mid-1970s at U.C. Berkeley on the merit of, not the demand for, angrily casting off authority, including scientific authority, or limits of any kind, in pursuit of sexual excess for its own sake.

Frequenting S&M themed gay bathhouses nightly, Foucault fueled among the brightest young minds the false justification for the increasingly impersonal and extreme sexual hedonism that overtook urban gay culture, a process that filtered down to dregs of the San Francisco's gay sex culture including in the form of his own person, in fact. In 1983, Foucault knew he had AIDS, but came back to San Francisco to revisit the leather bathhouse scene nightly, indifferent to spreading the HIV virus, until he died in 1984.

In his book, *Democratic Enlightenment* (2011), Princeton University's Jonathan Israel assails Foucault, in particular, for proposing to undermine the very humanist basis for the American revolution and any universal moral and democratic political foundations arising out of the Enlightenment, because Foucault held that "the primacy of reason was ultimately just a mask for the exercise of power." Foucault and postmodernism, generally, are fiercely against universal human rights, Israel argues, because any notion of universality is a form of oppression. This same influence informed the angry rejection of any authority, not only to ethics or accountability, but also to science or public health. As such, it fueled the preconditions and spread of the AIDS epidemic. Some contended that Foucault was a "saint" of the gay movement. He was more like a sinister purveyor of unspeakable misery and death who almost destroyed us, and still could.

Despite the venereal diseases ravaging gay scenes in the 1970s, no one saw AIDS coming, and the long incubation period meant that plenty of young men were doomed by exposure to the virus long before AIDS first manifested itself in the summer of 1981. The appearance of the HIV virus in urban gay communities could have been as early as 1974.

I was swept up in the urban gay scene in the early 1970s, after enthusiastically coming out and taking a leading role in the gay liberation movement of the San Francisco Bay Area. But it didn't take too long, or too much of all that promiscuous sex, for me to realize this was taking my life nowhere. I recall more than one opportunity for a serious romantic relationship that was shattered by the sheer volume of easy and casual sexual encounters in bathhouses, in parks, and dark rooms in the rear of bars. In New York there were the infamous long-haul trucks docked at the West Village piers that were stuffed full every night with men who were lucky if a struck match could enable them to catch a fleeting glimpse of some of the others they were performing sex with.

In S&M clubs, those preferred by the likes of Michel Foucault, the practice of "fisting" quickly evolved, spiking Crisco's market share, as well as gerbil adventures and public displays of things like "erotic vomiting." For all such behaviors, the scions of the gay movement – those profiting from the operation of clubs, baths, sex houses, poppers, intoxication and the proliferation of porn – argued that love and commitment may be out of the equation with all this, but it is replaced by boundless pleasure and "trust." For me, backing away from this scene was not easy. It involved a personal struggle having nothing to do with being prudish, but with wanting my life to matter for something. Because of the highly-addictive nature of the scene, there was no other way but effective exile. But while I loudly announced my departure from the political movement, I bounced along the urban scene's periphery, struggling with temptations, for years.

So, I was brutally abused by the force of those, like Foucault, who fueled the degeneration of the gay scene in this manner. As a young gay man, I was first abused by a culture that caused me to hate my orientation and to hide it at all cost. Coming out, I was abused by my family. My dad threatened to kill me, and I became *persona non grata* in my hometown. I turned to my gay community, but far from finding the love

I'd longed for, I found its polar opposite, violently determined to dash my hopes. In *The Normal Heart,* Larry Kramer's pitch is for love over impersonal sex, for gay lives with meaning and purpose over lives ruled by genitalia. Sad to say that for many, his message is still not getting through.

The cumulative influences of the modern hedonistic gay culture may be difficult to shake, especially given that much of it is a subset of modern, self-centered consumerist American culture generally. But grasping its sharp deviation from a better appreciation of our gay souls is a start.

PROPER CARE AND FEEDING

IN THE FINAL SECTIONS OF THIS effort my focus will be on the title of this one: our "proper care and feeding." In other words, how things ought to be for us, causing a creative tension between what is and what ought to be. I first coined the term, "gay soul," in a monograph, entitled "God and My Gay Soul," circulated in 1970 through the San Francisco Bay Area following my graduation for a master's degree with honors from theological seminary, my coming out, and my pioneering activism in the post-Stonewall Gay Liberation Front (all of which happened about the same time, if not exactly in that order). I have not seen a copy in 40 years, and while I have long forgotten what exactly I wrote about, I am certain it had to do with an affirmation of gay identity as an intentional and core component of creation.

While in seminary, the very progressive Pacific School of Religion affiliated with the equally progressive United Church of Christ denomination, perhaps the single most influential work we studied was Viktor Frankl's *Man's*

Search for Meaning (1946). Compiled during Dr. Frankl's imprisonment in a Nazi concentration camp and published with many updated editions after the war, it is a short work that embodies the essence of Frankl's theory and work as a therapist, even among the most despairing facing extermination in the concentration camps. As Rabbi Harold S. Kushner wrote in the introduction to the 1992 edition, one of Frankl's key ideas was that "life is not primarily a quest for pleasure, as Freud believed, or a quest for power, as Alfred Adler taught, but a quest for meaning." Frankl saw man as a "meaning-seeking creature," having three possible sources for meaning: "in work (doing something significant), in love (caring for another person) and in courage during difficult times." He believed that "forces beyond your control can take away everything you possess, except one thing, your freedom to choose how you will respond to the situation."

My life took a lot of twists and turns following seminary from coming out, being rejected by my family as a result, confronting and eventually recoiling from the radical hedonism that had taken over the gay culture, finding no apparent options but to align tangentially with a marginalized pro-socialist political entity that held me at arm's length because of my sexual orientation, living fearfully under the cloud of AIDS from the time it broke in the open in 1981 to when an antibody test was finally available in 1985, and then slowly reclaiming my life to, as I like to say, "do what any good gay boy would do," to use the gifts I'd first discovered in childhood to found in 1991 and since serve a community with a darned-good newspaper.

Looking back, I can say with confidence that my world view and approach to life did not deviate during that entire span until now from their core foundations in the teachings of Viktor Frankl.

Hence, I rejected the radical countercultural, nihilistic hedonism that took over gay culture in the 1970s, as I did rigid, cult-like authoritarian currents I found on the social margins, or in the growing selfish materialism of the overall American culture following the "Reagan revolution."

I've held to Frankl's three sources of meaning: in work, in love and in courage. If you want to know what's primarily animated this book, you've just found out.

Jonathan Sacks, the chief rabbi of Great Britain, authored a book, *The Great Partnership: God, Science and the Search for Meaning* (2011), which draws very heavily on Frankl's work but takes it further in an array of directions. While much could be said about this incredibly rich book, for purposes here, I note that Sacks adds to Frankl's notion that man is a "meaning-seeking" being with the supplementary notion that "man is a culture-producing animal." In both ways, mankind is distinct from all other forms of life, which means that we do not simply conform to any prevailing culture – such as what we have now – but that we are capable of, indeed we are challenged to, create a better culture.

Frankl identified man's inherent pursuit of meaning in life in three areas – in work, in love and in courage. Discovering what these mean for gay people constitutes our path forward for an altogether new and pioneering basis for gay identity, values and culture. They represent the vantage point from which, like a prophetic founder of a newly anointed tribe walking away from the burning ruins of a self-imploded village and not looking back, we can catch a glimpse of a bright horizon, freed from the shackles of degraded radical anarcho-hedonism, obsessive habits and addictions and the predatory rape and objectification of persons valued as nothing more than stimulants for insatiable lust.

Indeed, such a pilgrimage seems at present still more like stepping through a minefield in the midst of such collapsing conditions, and there also appears a seamless continuity of this distress through all contemporary culture, distinguishable only by matters of degree. So we gay people are having to do this for ourselves, using the likes of Frankl for guideposts, pioneering as well, perhaps, a rehabilitation of our entire culture. Such, in fact, has been our role through history.

In the grand scheme of things, we are here for a very important reason. Our same-sex erotic attraction is a creative binding force of nature as strong and purposeful as any in all creation, rooted in the empathic buffering glue that preserves, protects and advances civilizing influences, effectively steering evolution in the right direction. Our awakening from the sheer degradation and chaos mainstreamed into American culture by the social engineers of the "sex, drugs and rock and roll" counterculture of the late 1960s is a prelude and precondition for a revival of beneficent global culture, generally.

A fresh impulse for attaining and affirming enduring, personal hard-fought-for, face-to-face intimate human relationships, involving but not limited to the notion of gay marriage, reflects this awakening. Becoming significantly more self-conscious, this process can become socially transformative. By providing meaning through loving human connections, in Frankl's formula, marriage and intimate relationships inclusive of family and friends, grandmothers and lovers alike, function as stable platforms for enhancing the kind of empathy and kindness that reaches beyond comfort zones to uplift humanity generally. But they don't come easily. Our culture's demand for instant gratification notwithstanding, they all take work. But they are the cure for victims of sexual objectification, breaking through barriers imposed by lust-aroused mental, including electronic, fantasy images to see and engage real people and not just their "looks."

In San Francisco in the early 1970s, I walked past an attractive young man leaning against a storefront. Behind the storefront was one of the countless "peep show" joints where impersonal sex took place in the back. He gave me a typical "come hither" stare, but as I kept walking, I smiled and said, "Hi!" His face was instantly transformed by a huge grin that made his eyes sparkle. "Hi!," he beamed back. In that memorable case, a barrier of sexual objectification was broken to reach the real person inside, which as it turned out for him, was still right near the surface.

In too many other cases in gay ghettos those days, however, such real persons had receded to hard shells deep within. Everybody viewed everybody as a sexual object, and that was preached as the way it was supposed to be. Friendships were superficial, and in cases where "coming out" alienated family and old friendships, as in my case, leaving little in the way of genuine connections. Religion was no help. There were only two kinds: that which condemned homosexuality and that which affirmed it by uncritically endorsing the radical anarcho-hedonism dominating its culture. So, despite my seminary training, I found no place for me there.

But now, 40 years later, the push for gay marriage has embedded within it a potentially transformative, constructive affirmation of the meaning of persons generally that could save the very institution of marriage, itself, in our wider culture. It is not just about equal rights. Far more important is the relentless insistence on a social recognition of a sustainable relationship grounded in trust, faithfulness and commitment that goes to the very core of what it means to be human, and applying that to all relationships, marriage and beyond. Reactionaries hate gay marriage for more than its "same sex" aspect, but because it represents the notion that marriage should be a socially-affirmed bond and commitment of equals, and not composed of a dominant male and subordinate female and children. The reactionary's notion of the "nuclear family" is, indeed, sorely threatened by gay marriage. But theirs is destroying the institution because it undermines truly human intimacy for the sake of male dominion, to the detriment of everybody.

8

Gay Jesus?

THE PURPOSE OF THIS BOOK HAS been to determine and define a constructive, natural and purposeful role for gay people in the grand scheme of things, versus our existence as simply random or a corruption. I think it's working.

On the "Gay Jesus" question, there is nothing in the message or life of Jesus that contradicts a constructive nonconformist role for gays in the order of creation. Jesus' message and life are wholly compatible with the "third way" associated with the ancient Greek archetype of Prometheus, the one that stands between the hostile archetypes of stern law-abiding Apollo and selfish hedonist law-breaking Dionysus. Prometheus corresponds to nature's purpose for the existence of gay people. He is the giver of fire, the animated spirit of life itself, to mankind.

Distinct from male-dominated species reproduction and associated aggressive territorial dominion, gay Promethean love inflames the spirit through art, creativity, knowledge, humor and beauty in the cause of universal human empowerment.

In like kind, the life of Christ, as Oscar Wilde expressed it in his *De Profundis*, "is really an idyll," a poem, in which Christ "is the leader of all the lovers." Christ, Wilde wrote, "saw that love was the first secret of the world for which the wise men had been looking, and that it was only through love that one could approach either the heart of the leper or the feet of God."

The same core notion is embedded in currents of Judaism, through Philo, and Islam, through Ibn Sina. Just as Prometheus and Christ were cruelly punished by authoritarian, male dominated "powers that be" for kindling mankind's capacity for universal love, so those same powers have twisted, distorted and maligned the images and messages of Prometheus and Christ over the centuries. Some of the worst distortions have been within the church, itself, from Apollonian and Dionysian sides.

On the Apollonian side, idolatry substitutes for Christ where Protestant fundamentalism primarily worships a book and Catholicism its institutions. The earliest church, influenced by (our) Plato, saw Christ's message and life as an "incarnation" of the causal purpose of creation (God), being "consubstantial" with it. As such, Christ was seen as the "Logos" (in Greek, "Word") of the Gospel of John, the second person of the Trinity. But fundamentalists, who hold to the bizarre, magic notion that the Bible is inerrant, the literal word-for-word of God, in practice assign the role of the "Logos" not to the message and life of Christ, but to the Bible. They pervert a "Trinitarian" notion of "God, Christ and Holy Spirit," substituting "God, Bible and Holy Spirit," allowing whomever claims to embody the Holy Spirit (any charlatan) to wave the Bible, quote from any passage, and claim he speaks for God, including by condemning gay people to hell.

On the Dionysian side, "consubstantiality" is undermined in a different way, dismissing the message and life of Christ in favor of a reckless and self-serving interpretation often designed to negate guilt associated with excessive hedonism. The moral suasion of the progressive church peaked in the ministry of Dr. Martin Luther King, Jr. But following his assassination in 1968 and the flood of hedonistic "sex, drugs and rock and roll" counterculture influences that ensued, the liberal church fell strangely silent.

I do not contend that gay people alone express the kind of love that the ancient Greek titan Prometheus exhibited by stealing fire from Mt. Olympus and giving to mankind, fire interpreted as love that inflames the human spirit. But I feel strongly that within our wider humanity, gay people have always been a prevalent and indispensable component of that inflammation process, so to speak. Throughout human history, gays have manifested a higher and more potent love than the procreative impulse, their love directed toward protecting and advancing the empowerment of those otherwise subservient to brutal straight-male dominion. Nature has empowered gay love with intense erotic and heroic impulses to achieve this work, to courageously withstand dominant culture, and to carry out its mission even if no fulfillment of modern notions of gay sexual expression occur.

We've been around since the very beginning and, if silently and secretly, in far, far greater numbers than anyone imagines or any historical record, even to the present day, can account for.

In line with the Promethean archetype (as opposed to legalistic Apollonian or hedonistic Dionysian ones, as outlined by Nietzsche and Freud), every evidence in the Biblical record is that the historical Jesus of Nazareth had at the center of his message and life a form of a Promethean "fire giving" of universal love and humble, compassionate creative work to mankind. His parables, such as of the Good Samaritan and the Pharisee and the Publican, demonstrate this, as does the entire Sermon on the Mount that includes the profound simplicity of the Lord's Prayer. Such passages reflect the authentic "voice" of the historical Jesus, as my revered professor of New Testament theology while in seminary, Dr. Joachim Jeremias, established so eloquently. Dr. Jeremias is credited with identifying the importance of Jesus' speaking in Aramaic, his native tongue, the word, "Abba," translated more like a child's familiar "Daddy," rather than "Father," to refer to God.

That word reflects Jesus' call to "become like little children," to tap into native Promethean fire, a natural inclination to love non-judgmentally and feel passion for the beauty of life, itself, sensibilities that otherwise tend, in the course of acclimation into rote and legalistic male-dominated society, to become blunted or extinguished. As our own magnificent Oscar Wilde, not a religious man, wrote in *De Profundis* while in prison, "Far off, like a perfect pearl, one can see the city of God. It is so wonderful that it seems as if a child could reach it on a summer's day. And so a child could." Such is the Kingdom of God that is aglow within one, as Christ proclaimed. Wilde described Christ as "a lover for whose love the whole world was too small," and wrote of his miracles that "such was the charm of his personality that his mere presence could bring peace to souls in anguish, and that those who touched his garments or his hands forgot their pain."

"People who had seen nothing of life's mystery, saw it clearly, and others who had been deaf to every voice but that of pleasure heard for the first time the voice of love," he wrote, such that "evil passions fled at his approach and men whose dull unimaginative lives had been but a mode of death rose as it were from the grave when he called them; or that when he taught on the hillside the multitude forgot their hunger and thirst and cares for the world, and that to his friends who listened to him as he sat at meal the coarse food seemed delicate, and the water had the taste of good wine."

"He had pity," Wilde wrote, "for the poor, for those who are shut up in prisons, for the lowly, for the wretched," but also "for the rich, for the hard hedonists, for those who waste their freedom in becoming slaves to things. ...Who knew better than he that it is vocation and not volition that determines us?" Christ understood "the leprosy of the leper, the darkness of the blind, the fierce misery of those who live for pleasure, the strange poverty of the rich," Wilde wrote. "He awakens in us that temper of wonder to which romance always appeals." For him, "every moment should be beautiful. ...His morality is all sympathy, just what morality should be." By describing Christ this way, Wilde did not win the favor of the church, because to him Christ was a poet, and his life poetry. Wilde criticized organized religion, writing, "Endless repetition, in and out of season, has spoiled for us the freshness, the naivete, the simple romantic charm of the Gospels. ...All repetition is anti-spiritual." But the true revelation of this genuinely inspired work of Wilde lay in his identification of his own gay soul with the soul of Christ, the universal soul of the life-giving Promethean.

De Profundis, identifying with Christ's universal love, himself (and thereby, as implied, from the standpoint of his identity as a gay man), sat well with no one. Wilde's admirers were dismayed by the deeply spiritual nature of the work, attributing it to the degradation of prison life, and church leaders had even less interest in his unconventional, radically humanitarian appreciation of Christ. But the work was a fuller exposition of themes Wilde presented in earlier works, especially *The Picture of Dorian Gray*, where he drew a sharp distinction between the hedonistic pursuit of pleasure for its own sake and true happiness. In *De Profundis*, he wrote about "the note of doom that like a purple thread runs through the texture of *Dorian Gray*." Embracing such a perspective on life, including his own gay life, Wilde remained a happy soul until his untimely death, contrary to the popular view that, after prison, he was penniless, depressed and doomed to ignominy in Paris. His close lifelong friend, Robbie Ross, insisted it was quite otherwise, and it was Ross who saw to the publication of *De Profundis* following Wilde's death.

If flamboyant and filled with wry and ironic humor, Wilde's life and work was completely contrary in its sentiment and intent to the outrageous misrepresentation by Neil McKenna in his book, *The Secret Life of Oscar Wilde* (2005). McKenna dared to falsely assert that Wilde wrote *Dorian*

Gray to seduce readers into the hedonistic excesses of the London underworld.

So it is with British playwright Alan Bennett (who penned *The History Boys*), who performed a hatchet job on three important gay creative giants, poet W. H. Auden, composer Benjamin Britten and author Thomas Mann, in his *The Habit of Art* (2009). To Bennett, there exists no nobility or virtue in gay sensibility. He recognizes only thinly-veiled social constraints on vulgar hedonistic, predatory lust. Whatever it may suggest about his own gay life, such a conviction reveals a jaded inability to appreciate how creative genius can focus the compassionate gay impulse on great, loving achievements, including the uplifting and edification of objects of affection, rather than their defilement.

The Habit of Art details the lives and careers of its main characters Auden and Britten (and the oft-referenced Mann). But it treats their interest in adolescents as simply open or barely repressed craving, rather than a creator's love of their potential. Thus, to Bennett's mind, the subjects of their interest are, just beneath the surface, objects to be devoured by lust, rather than recipients of a gay love whose creative energy strives to free them from the stranglehold of male-dominated straight society, and to transform them into loving creative individuals, in turn.

But the greatest slander of *The Habit of Art* is contained in its title, that creative geniuses consider their work matters of mere "habit." The rent boy in *The Habit of Art* sounds off at the end, demanding of Auden, "When do we figure and get to say our say?...When do we take our bow?...We... the fodder of art? … I want to know." Auden sighs, "We can't help you."

In the play, that was pretty much the sum of it. In reality, as a compassionate, loving gay genius, the entire purpose of Auden's life and creative work was, actually, to answer precisely the opposite.

Born This Way

The hit single, *Born This Way*, by Lady Gaga – the enormously-talented Stefani Germanotta – is a huge, obvious "shout out" to gays, a big component of her following. It was her contribution to the "It Gets Better" offensive against bullying and hate that resulted from a spate of high-profile teen gay suicides in the fall of 2010. But her *Born This Way* anthem can also be extended to Gaga, herself, as one who exhibited enormous talent at a young age, beginning piano at age four, writing a ballad by 13, and bringing her portable keyboard to sing at gay clubs and other venues in Manhattan's Lower East side as a 14-year-old. Despite her flamboyant style and staging, at her core she's phenomenally skilled, with a good heart, to boot. *Born This Way*, for her, refers to her musical inclination and empathetic sensibility. That's also the "This Way" that defines what sets gays apart in our early years, as well, the root of our most precious and critical contributions to humanity.

Little depicts this better than the amazing *Billy Elliot* story, both as Lee Hall's Academy Award-nominated screenplay for the 2000 film version, and as the stage version, *Billy Elliot the Musical* which debuted in 2005 in London, and has played worldwide before audiences totaling 7.5 million to date, and counting. In the musical version, which won 10 Tony Awards, including Best Musical, upon arriving on Broadway, Hall's story and lyrics are augmented by Elton John's music. The story is about a youth growing up in British mine country during the historic British Mine Workers' strike in the 1980s, who at age 11 discovers and seeks to pursue his natural affinity for ballet against pressures from his family, community and the strife-ridden times. In the musical, it opens to "The Stars Look Down" sung by a chorus of mine workers, affirming a cosmic dimension to the story.

The movie version, starring Jamie Bell, begins with young Billy using his bed as a trampoline while listening to T-Rex singing "I danced myself right out of the womb" (*Cosmic Dancer*).

The story resonates strongly with gays who as youths found themselves with dispositions contrary to the norm (myself included). In a straight-male dominated conformist world where boys like sports and girls like dolls, inclinations toward other, nonconformist interests usually encounter resistance.

Gay screenwriter Todd Haynes in his brilliant film, V*elvet Goldmine* (1998), has his own colorful way of depicting the "otherness" of our tribe in its opening segment. The baby Oscar Wilde, the famous gay "pop idol" of his day, arrives in a space ship and is planted on a doorstep in a basket with an emerald pin attached to his blanket. The subject of the *Velvet Goldmine* story (granted, this is how I view it) is the emerald pin, its passing on from one bearer to the next. In 1955, 55 years after Wilde's death, the pin appeared in the dirt to a lad whose bloodied face had just been planted there by bullies in a school yard.

That lad grows up to be Jack Fairy, who Haynes describes in the interview by Owen Moverman which appears as a preface to the published screenplay, "remains the kind of lost originator of the whole glam thing," who is "the 'real' thing." (The movie is ostensibly about the glam rock craze of the early 1970s, when gay liberation exploded). Jack Fairy comes home with the emerald pin and, according to the screen direction, "Clasps the emerald pin to his shirt, stops in front of the mirror and looks up. Jack's lip is still bleeding. He touches it. Gently, he rubs the blood over his lips like lipstick." Then a female voice-over says, "Jack would discover that somewhere there were others quite like him, singled out for a great gift. And one day...the whole stinking world would be theirs."

In the film, Jack Fairy is a marginal figure, appearing only at the beginning and at the end. But with his "instinctive need to camp it up" (according to Haynes) he kicks off the glam rock fad, which is then carried to fame by the film's main character, Brian Slade (played by Jonathan Rhys Meyers), a David Bowie-type figure. While Brian Slade tries out a same-sex relationship with the character Curt Wild (Ewan McGregor), an Iggy Pop-type, it's not real for him, just as his musical act is not Jack Fairy's "real thing." Slade soon arranges for his own disappearance.

But Slade's music and erotic same-sex on-stage antics nonetheless awaken the gay spirit of another player, the journalist character Arthur Stuart (Christian Bale). Thus, the emerald pin is passed behind, so to speak, the main action in the film from Fairy to Stuart, from the one "real thing" to another. Beneath or behind the fad lay the passing of the emerald pin, the marker of our authentic gay tribe, we who are "singled out for a great gift."

The film accurately depicts both the meteoric rise and, through Brian Slade's figure, the rapid crash of the post-Stonewall gay liberation scene. While Fairy and Stuart are genuine emerald pin-bearing gays, the ranks of youths pouring into the glam rock scene were swollen massively by a new social encouragement to play with gay sexuality. It became a countercultural imperative to engage in as much sex with as many partners as possible, which soon turned the gay movement from a beautiful liberating experience for gays into a compulsive drug and sex addicted, disease-crawling urban nightmare.

Asking, "What does it mean to be gay?," I identified three ways in which same-sex erotic attraction is linked to a preponderance of personal qualities of great benefit to humanity. Using self-reflection as a measure, I've identified these qualities in countless gays I've encountered, even if they don't apply to everyone.

RECAPPING GAY SENSIBILITY

FIRST, GAY SENSIBILITY IS A HEIGHTENED empathy and compassion often manifested in early childhood by sympathizing with underdogs and discovering talents that bring happiness to others. Second, "alternate sensual perspective" is an inclination to be drawn to something other, not just erotically but also aesthetically, than the majority. Third, "constructive nonconformity," is the inclination to invent, create or represent a different course than passive conformity in life, in a loving, constructive way.

Amplifying and valuing these qualities away from lust for hard bodies can call into being all that gays have had, through the centuries, to bring to the betterment of society and themselves. Uplifting these qualities in our culture, out from the radical anarcho-hedonism of the 1970s that still dominates it, can empower our cultural reinvention based on genuine human relations rooted in the meaning that people derive from their work, their loves and their courage

Everything beautiful that humanity brings to the world comes from beautiful souls. All have a capacity for beauty, but too many ignore that for selfish instant gratification. The entire culture suffers from this, and it will take many beautiful self-actualized gay souls to heal it. I am blessed to have many wonderfully creative, accomplished and beautiful gay friends. Two, well-known openly-gay, extraordinary national treasures, Don Bachardy and Johnny Weir are different in many ways. There's a 50-year difference in age and a continent of difference in location. Their talents are different, but therein lies their first great commonality: both have striven relentlessly in their lives to cultivate and present their talents as gifts to humanity, Bachardy as a portrait artist in Southern California, Weir as a figure skater in New York. Bachardy, born in 1934, was the long-time companion of the British-born writer Christopher Isherwood, who was declared by his great friend, the late Gore Vidal, as "the best prose writer in English." Bachardy, under Isherwood's loving patronage, trained to become a prominent artist in his own right, doing portraits of all manner of celebrities and important people, including the official rendering of Gov. Jerry Brown that hangs in the California state capital. Weir, born in 1984, is a three-time U.S. figure skating champion and two time U.S. Olympic contender currently training for a third Olympic run.

Both have tons written both about and by them. In Bachardy's case, Isherwood devoted more ink to him in his posthumously-published diaries than anyone else by far. Bachardy has published his own material, too, including *Stars in My Eyes* (2000), a catalog of his portraits with personal remembrances of 33 famous people. Weir published a memoir of the first 26 years of his life entitled, *Welcome to My World* (2010) that is intelligent, candid and worthwhile. Weir's successes, failures, controversies and irrepressible flamboyance have landed boatloads of ink and celluloid in newspapers, tabloids and reality TV shows.

I had up-close, intense one-on-one encounters with both when I first met them in person. I met Weir in March 2004 after he'd won his first national championship. Watching him on TV in January, I wrote in my diary (as I recently rediscovered) that his winning long program was so poetic, emotive, graceful and soaring that it was "what my soul looks like." I used my newspaper credentials to arrange an interview at his Newark, Delaware home rink on March 11, and we sat across from each other, face-to-face in a practice room for over an hour, a session that included a rather creative photo shoot at the end.

When you engage someone that intently, you can see far into them. I encountered Johnny Weir's resolve to speak the truth with intelligence and articulation, to achieve, and above all, to be himself. So, he'd responded to his Russian coach's urging "to remember the art and beauty, and forget the pettiness of scores." He saw his insistence on doing things his own, if unusual, way to be standing in solidarity with every kid that's ever been treated as an outcast for being different from the norm.

I knew about Don Bachardy before I met him at his home overlooking the Santa Monica canyon to interview him and have him paint a portrait of me. The portrait painting had the same intense, one-on-one engagement as my interview with Weir. It took almost three hours. As he gazed back at him while he looked into details of my face, my eyes and my soul, I caught a glimpse of what Isherwood saw in him which made it worth working so hard for their relationship to last.

NOT ASSIMILATIONIST, BUT TRANSFORMATIVE

"THOUGH OUTWARDLY WE ARE WASTING AWAY, yet inwardly we are being renewed day by day." This quote from Paul's second letter to the Corinthians (4:16) in the Bible describes the exact opposite of Oscar Wilde's *The Picture of Dorin Gray*, where the inward person wasted away while the outward one remained young and beautiful. Wilde's reversal of order was clearly intentional, a harsh critique of the philosophy of hedonism raging in his day. This also describes modern urban gay culture to a tee. This culture's fixation is on the "tyranny of hard bodies," and its norm is to waste hours a day at a gym, working tirelessly to forestall aging and "love handles," while any impulse to cultivate the mind and spirit are blurred by nightly intoxication and shallow obsession with acts of impersonal sex performed on the outward flesh of others.

Gay academic David Halperin's book, *How to Be Gay* (2012), based on his course at the University of Michigan by the same name, is a shameless, wholesale tribute to this urban gay male culture. It suggests that anyone failing to comply with the accepted icons of this culture is somehow less than really gay.

Halperin's 1995 book, *Saint Foucault*, was the take off point for my original Gay Science series, with my first three installments entitled, *St. Foucault, Are You Kidding?* So it is apropos as I prepare to conclude that I address Halperin's latest fiction. I hold "sexologist" philosopher Michel Foucault (1926-1984) in vile contempt. His influence in San Francisco in the 1970s as a lecturer at U.C. Berkeley not only contributed to the outbreak of AIDS, but made it impossible for me to realize my gay identity within the radical anarcho-hedonist gay culture he helped shape.

Ironically, I could realize my gay soul only by resisting that gay culture. I backed away from its descent into madness (such as its stubborn refusal to deter the spread of AIDS), and was fortunate to find sanctuary in a sequence of intimate, reciprocal loving relationships, my most important one persisting from 1983 to the present. Halperin's new book mentions nothing of the downsides of urban gay male culture, with no talk of alcoholism, career-stagnation, drug abuse, sexually-transmitted diseases or suicide. He goes so far as to contend that AIDS and the 600,000 gay male lives it took in the U.S. alone "a terrible historical accident, and it had nothing to do with us." But who infected all those beautiful gay souls, even after, like Foucault, they knew they were killing their sex partners? To begin to honestly address our gay culture, we have to begin with fact, not convenient fiction.

'WHAT NOW, LAZARUS?'

ON GAY PRIDE SUNDAY, JUNE 13, 2010, marking the 40th anniversary of the first Gay Pride parade, I had the honor of delivering remarks to those assembled a few blocks from the Pride festival at the First Congregational Church in downtown Washington, D.C. I titled my remarks, "What Now Lazarus?," drawing from the question a seminary professor put to me long ago. The Biblical figure Lazarus was raised from the dead, but there is no account of what he did after that. "Did he go back to growing dates, or did he make something more of his life?," my adroit professor asked. I applied that question to the gay movement today. We have been raised from the dead, metaphorically, in three ways: from the oppression of our closets, from the terrible AIDS epidemic, and, soon, from second-class status in the eyes of the law (while huge fights still need to be fought against a lot of persisting bigotry and hate, this is inevitable). After all this, then what?

Do we assimilate into the male-dominated, profoundly unequal and militaristic prevailing society, becoming as stupid TV sitcoms or right-wing scions seeking to co-opt us would have it, absorbed into and indistinguishable from all that? Do we angrily repudiate assimilation with radical, post-modern "queer theories" and behaviors that define us in terms of perpetual rage? Or do we follow the alternative approach that has been the subject of this book?

This alternative is consistent with what history shows are core expressions of our naturally inherent and vitally important gay souls. Preponderant qualities of heightened empathy and compassion for the underdog, of an alternate sensual perspective (our same-sex erotic attraction being a natural derivative of humanity's powerful impulse for empathy and not a variant of the drive for species reproduction) applied to all aspects of life, and a constructive non-conformity account for the amazing contributions our "tribe" has brought to the benefit of all humanity for thousands of years. Contrary to the shallow conceits of current, hedonistic urban gay culture, we gay souls have been a major, constructive factor in civilization since before the beginning. Sensitive to the plight of women, children, the elderly and downtrodden in savage patriarchal male chauvinist, war-mongering cultures, we worked to build the institutions over eons that have advanced compassion over cruelty, science over superstition, beauty over corruption and equality over tyranny.

We, with our natural feminist allies (and our natural inclination to identify and align with strong women struggling in all stations in life), sparked the American revolution as an epochal blow against the male-chauvinist right of monarchies to hereditary succession, and built a constructive alternative in the U.S. Constitution's framework for fair and just governance that had embedded within it what has slowly progressed to equal rights under the law for everybody. The enormously positive new development of the post-Stonewall era has been our increasing capacity to "come out," gaining for us a degree of personal integrity before the world that was always denied before. It promises to result in an explosion of our creativity and beneficial role to society as a whole, although that was stalled by the radical, anarcho-hedonism imposed on our urban culture in the 1970s that devolved into the AIDS horror and stubbornly persists to this day in urban centers.

But now, the successful fight for marriage represents for us a fresh constructive front in the struggle for full human equality, not just because we have the right to it, but more importantly, because gay marriage advances the notion of loving bonds of equals, striking another blow against the male supremacist paradigm. Some who favor it on gay rights grounds alone may overlook this. Like Lazarus in the Bible, gay souls have been raised from the tomb of the closet, of AIDS, and second-hand citizen status to a purpose, to the meaning in life we derive through dedication to our creative work, our love and our courage on behalf of humanity, as a whole.

Our gay liberation will be complete only when all humanity enjoys the benefits of the same kind of life, liberty and the pursuit of happiness we set as our purpose long, long ago.

9

Prometheans

FOR GAY MEN DURING THE AIDS Dark Age (1981-1996), during which time an estimated 400,000 of us died horribly and way too soon, there was nothing more valued than life, itself, and as Prior, the main character in Tony Kushner's amazing play about that era, *Angels in America* insists on, "Life…more life!"

In this 1993 epic Pulitzer, Tony and Emmy Award winning play, subtitled "A Gay Fantasia on National Themes," life is the reality most affirmed in the seven-hour (presented in two separate parts) drama about struggling to cope in the AIDS Dark Age. The play is about insisting upon life while confused angels counsel against the idea, and ends with its AIDS-wracked but still standing hero Prior blessing all of us at the healing pond of the angel Bethesda – this one not in Jerusalem, but Central Park – and by so doing bestowing life upon us.

The promise of "life, liberty (liberation) and the pursuit of happiness" as "inalienable rights" involves not only enjoying them, but empowerment to provide them to others, as well (something we homosexuals are very good at). It's because the promise was not only written, but delivered by the Founding Fathers, who made a revolution to secure it for all. Each of its components – life, liberty and happiness – is properly defined in terms of the other two.

Drawing the exhaustive *Angels in America* to a close – after God is absent, angels are befuddled as heaven is crumbling, a Jewish activist prays for her enemy, a Mormon mother makes a breakthrough and puts love ahead of everything, a saucy male nurse steals from the rich for a friend in need, a depressed housewife breaks free, Prior breaks a fever, and much more – as I just quoted above, Prior turns from his friends sitting at the Bethesda fountain to speak to the audience, to us homosexuals. He says:

> The fountain is not flowing now, they turn it off in the winter, ice in the pipes. But in the summer it's a sight to see. I want to be around to see it. I plan to be. I hope to be.
> This disease will be the end of many of us, but not nearly all, and the dead will be commemorated and will struggle on with the living, and we are not going away. We don't die secret deaths anymore. The world only spins forward. We will be citizens. The time has come.
> Bye now. You are fabulous creatures, each and every one. And I bless you: More Life. The Great Work Begins.

For non-gays asking, "What about us?," this play is not about them, but for homosexuals in our darkest hours. Others can watch and learn. Especially for any homosexuals, and our friends and loved ones who lived in that era, *Angels in America* is amazing beyond words. It was made into an HBO mini-series in 2003 that won an astounding 11 Emmys (directed by Mike Nichols and with a star-studded cast that included Al Pacino, Meryl Streep, Emma Thompson, Patrick Wilson and Mary-Louise Parker). An overarching theme is the unspoken alliance between women and gays against white male brutes, with the brutes in the play – the notorious Roy Cohn and his young lawyer ally – both being right-wing closet queens. Their closets are the product of the straight white male dominated culture that they bought into, and by so doing brought misery upon others. (Such gay assimilationists become, practically speaking in life, political reactionaries because assimilation doesn't come naturally to them. They have worked hard at it.)

This points to the role of homosexuals in nature's wider order, to protect and provide for the advance of civilization by allying with independent-minded women to resist the cruelty and brutality of unbridled male supremacist behavior.

The archetypal male supremacist order is death-centered. Territorial by nature, it raises its young to fight its wars and to generate more fodder. Young males are raised to kill and die, or spiritually die to the monotony of its convention, and young females to bury them, actually and metaphorically, and make more. Core homosexual traits – heightened sensibility, alternate perspective and constructive non-conformity

– resist the dynamics of this archetype, combining with awakened women to fight it by…giving life!

Life in this sense – not as birthing to fuel the machinations of death, but a life that flares up and empowers the human spirit – is fundamental to who we are as homosexuals. We collaborate with women to break the death-cycle of male supremacy and create great, just and enlightened civilizations. Our power to give this life – through humor, irony, education, music, dance, art, poetry and invention – is compromised only when we lose a passion for it. Thus, it's so critical to fight against resignation and jaded cynicism and insist on this life in Angels in America.

Our heightened empathy, alternate sensual perspective and constructive non-conformity – that have combatted through history the kind of male chauvinist anarcho-hedonism that condones, sometimes encourages rape. This was rampant in the right wing so-called "counterculture" that swept through the fledgling post-Stonewall gay movement in the late 1960s and 1970s, the perverse and twisted offspring of the 19th-century German philosopher Friedrich Nietzsche's "superman" and his "will to power." Nietzsche's cosmology involved man's struggle between Appollonian and Dionysian opposites, between obedience to laws out of a sense of duty and the wanton abandonment of them in the pursuit of pure pleasure. The Nietzschean superman" conquers social convention on behalf of his true self, his Dionysian impulse, his "will to power."

Such a system justified the worst, most brutal excesses of the 20th century, particularly the rise of fascism in Germany and its systematic genocide of innocents. It also informed the "counterculture's" efforts to undermine morally-grounded sensibility with a savage pursuit of relentless, lawless hedonism. Systematic rape and child abuse were endemic to the so-called "sexual revolution" of that era. It was almost as if the whole movement had been precipitated by predators to alienate the young from their families and then to snare them when they headed to the urban centers for their "summers of love" and yearnings for freedom. I fought against it as long as I could.

PROMETHEUS UNBOUND

THE CORE IDENTITY DEFINING OUR HOMOSEXUAL tribe is, in terms of archetypes taken from Greek mythology, not Dionysian in nature, but Promethean. This has important implications for every gay person. Dionysus was the god whose archetype represents pleasure-seeking hedonistic excess. Prometheus was the Titan who stole fire from Mt. Olympus and gave it to man, who also provided man with the "arts of civilization," science, mathematics, agriculture, writing and medicine. In fact, in some ancient mythological accounts, he is attributed with the very creation of the human race. In the post-Stonewall gay movement, Dionysian anarcho-hedonism came to define gays and our culture. As set against the Greek archetype of the god Apollo, who represented authoritative order and structure of the dominant, conformist culture, Dionysus was touted as the anti-culture. Dionysus marked the rebellion against the status quo that acted out in the form of "sexual freedom" and the radically-excessive, impersonal, addictive sex that came to dominate urban gay subcultures.

We know how this came to drive the post-Stonewall movement into the ground, resulting in over 400,000 self-inflicted deaths from AIDS. While Dionysus persists to this day as the dominant paradigm defining the gay community, among other things enabled by those who profit from it, this identity did not arise from within our tribe. As I have documented, it was imposed by, and imported from, the right wing "sex, drugs and rock and roll" so-called "counterculture" that arose in the 1960s. Gays are not naturally Dionysian, but succumb to such tendencies when pressures arise from dominating cultural influences. In the U.S., self-centered, pleasure-seeking Dionysian "rebellion" has increasingly dominated the entire cultural landscape of individual lives since the rise of "consumerism" in the 1950s. It's led to today's serious epidemic of Internet-fueled sex addiction akin to what urban gays experienced so intensely in the 1970s, with the consequential "emotional curtains" that such addictions draw down within victims, causing "intimacy disorders," crippling abilities to relate in loving ways to others.

The prevailing straight Apollonian-archetype male-chauvinist, patriarchal over-culture, and Dionysian rebellion under-culture are flip sides of the same coin. This was the view of the 19th century German philosopher Friedrich Nietzsche. He posed the double-sided notion of the Apollonian-Dionysian struggle in his book, *The Birth of Tragedy* (1872), claiming that human "existential being" is defined by this tension. But this doesn't apply to the natural disposition of gays, whose distinguishing characteristics suggest a "third way." Nietzsche and major currents of modern culture fail to acknowledge this, although ironically it has played a massive role in the development of civilization and notions underlying the American experience.

Prometheus is the mythical figure whose archetype has been compared to that of Jesus of Nazareth in the Biblical tradition. He sacrificed himself in order to serve humankind, to provide it with fire (the spark inflaming the human spirit), science, the arts and learning. Hungarian scholar Carl Kerenyi, in his 1946 book, *Prometheus: Archetypal Image of Human Existence* (part of a series published by the Princeton University Press), claims the Prometheus-Jesus correlation breaks down because Prometheus was a god and not also "fully man." But that seems a flimsy deference to religious authority, because the myths of ancient Greek gods were allegories co-mingled with oral histories in which gods were more properly glorified legends and heroes.

The sensibilities unique to gay people I've explored in this book include a heightened empathy, an alternative sensual perspective and a constructive non-conformity. As our early pioneer Andre Gide wrote in his Socratic dialogues on the purposefulness and natural basis for same-sex erotic attraction called *Corydon* (1920), because we gays question nature from a different viewpoint, nature gives us different answers.

The "different viewpoint and different answers" define us. They have compelled us toward a form of constructive nonconformity that has stood for eons against Apollonian male-dominated culture, which at its core is territorial and brutal in its treatment of women and children as chattel and slaves in the maintenance and expansion of territories. By putting fire (the spirit of human empowerment), science and

204   EDUCATION OF A GAY SOUL

art into the hands of humanity, in general, and not restricting it to the province of the dominant Zeus-like males, the Promethean interrupts male-dominated culture on behalf of a more egalitarian, compassionate culture. He and she are revolutionaries interceding on behalf of the oppressed to move humanity forward through enlightenment.

The great heroes of our long history, from the psalmist, tyrant-slayer, lover of Jonathan and king, David of the Old Testament, to the fathers of progressive western thought and morals, Socrates and Plato, and key founders and defenders of the American republic, Hamilton, Lincoln, Whitman and Eleanor Roosevelt, all reflect this powerful archetype. We are Promethean nation builders, not Dionysian hedonists.

The novel discovery made over the course of these chapters is that the archetype identifying the proper role of gay people in history smashes modern culture's straight-jacketed, commonly-accepted dualism of Apollonian (law abiding) versus Dionysian (law breaking) with a "third way." The "third way" is Promethean, the notion of those with heightened empathy and compassion for humanity, passionately driven by an alternative perspective about the prevailing order of things, and engaged in a constructive nonconformity, defying the existing order on behalf of mankind. Those characteristics define Prometheus, the Titan god of ancient Greek mythology, who stole fire from Olympus to give it and much more to mankind, and they also define, as I have articulated in these chapters, the core characteristics of historic gay identity and personality.

It is delightfully astonishing that the rediscovery of Promethean gay identity, after thousands of years, comes now, in the wake of the Stonewall reawakening of the full potential of gay persons in the shaping of culture. This is lawful, after all. The last time gays played the kind of open role in a society as we are claiming now was in ancient Greece. In those days, the Promethean connection to gay sensibility did not need to be explicitly tied to same-sex erotic attraction, because the latter was such an accepted factor in the social norms of the time.

Still, the Promethean was understood to suffer for his and her gifts to mankind. In the myth, Prometheus is punished by Zeus (the archetypal figure symbolizing straight-male dominant society) for his work on behalf of mankind by being tied to a rock where an eagle, the symbol of Zeus' authority, came to eat out his liver every day. The notion of having one's liver torn out, and regrown, on a daily basis, corresponds to the tolls, emotional and otherwise, so many of us pay for being gay.

So, after 3,000 years, gay people are poised for the first time to regain the mantle of the Promethean archetype, and by so doing, shedding the erroneous and destructive Dionysian (pleasure-seeking "outlaw") archetype heaped upon us by straight male-dominated culture.

Many gays seek to shift their archetypal identity away from Dionysian, especially given the cataclysm of sexual excesses that led to AIDS, by pursuing the Apollonian archetype – that is, seeking to conform and assimilate within the cultural parameters of violent straight-male dominated society.

Now, however, we can see ourselves as constructively nonconformist, as Prometheans with our own distinct, important identity in the wider social order, neither Apollonian or Dionysian.

What are some implications? For one, we must reconsider our history in ways I've proposed. Instead of looking for explicit same-sex activity to cite evidences of us, we instead look for evidences of Promethean impulses and behavior, knowing that opportunities for same-sex activity have been overwhelmingly repressed, or expressed only in licentious forms, for eons. It means reinventing our gay history in this way, starting by eliminating entirely "post-Stonewall reductionism" from scholarship.

For another, we can define our sensible creative proclivities in terms of the Promethean archetype, on the one hand, and define the Promethean archetype on the basis of our sensible creative proclivities, on the other. For example, the ancient Prometheus' gift to mankind of fire represents not only invention and civilization, but the animating spark that inflames human souls (in some myths, in fact, Prometheus actually created mankind). Every act that fuels and enlarges the fire animating human souls, then, is Promethean. There is nothing that gay people are inclined to do more than fuel fires of human souls! Offering encouragement, selfless generosity, optimism through tears, gifts of beauty, song, comedy, camp and laughter as well as science, medicine, art and design, these are core characteristics of our tribe, and they're all Promethean.

The hallmark of Promethean nature is a dedication to excellence and achievement that everyone on that stage demonstrated. When we embrace our true Promethean identity, we don't just do good deeds, we aspire to them, and are driven to pursue them. Not that we don't seek reciprocal romance. But nature uses same-sex erotic attraction as a social glue, binding persons of the same sex, often not reciprocally, alas, but to make a better, more humane society, overall. We are naturally inclined to provide a kind of love that is too often not returned in kind. Thus, our livers are eaten out daily. Such may be our destiny, but remember also that Prometheus was eventually freed by a handsome young god-man Hercules.

It is fair to ask, in response to my proposition that the gay Promethean archetype represents "constructive non-conformity," who defines "constructive." Does it come from some authoritarian source defining it for us? When asked that question once regarding my Gay Science series which had been published weekly starting October 2010 in the web edition of my *Falls Church News-Press* and reprinted on the pages of the superb Metro Weekly gay news magazine in Washington, D.C, I replied:

> "I say no one decides. It comes from within the individual, as has been the whole point of my series. The individual discovers an impulse within him or her that can be called empathy which seeks the well-being of others.
>
> "This leads to a desire to learn how that can best be achieved, which leads to an appreciation of how one's own individual gifts can contribute. From the standpoint of erotic attraction to the same sex, this places an added emphasis on the well-being of persons

of the same sex, something hierarchical male dominated straight society does not permit or offer to either sex.

"Yes, it is all derived from empathy, nature's tool for our survival and the unfolding of our full enfranchisement and potential. In the old days, we could call it love, but that word is so out of fashion these days."

Prometheus, in the ancient Greek myth, was punished by Zeus (the archetype of straight male dominated culture) for stealing fire, reason and other benefits to give to mankind. He was punished because of his "excessive love for man" and defiant refusal to "quit his man-loving disposition." In so doing, he "did not tremble at the name of Zeus." He was defined by his "excessive love for man" in defiance of the straight male dominated cultural model. Such is the paradigm for our gay identity.

Love, or empathy, is a natural human predisposition that we gays do not limit to the dominant culture's accepted norms, but experience as a natural defiance of them. But it is not a negative, angry defiance. It is a passionate, often erotic desire to present mankind with the gift of fire in the form of a creative expression that powers and inflames human souls to become Promethean, themselves. Empathy is contained in each "unit of action" of human development, and identity derived from the succession of them. Empathy is a form of direct connectivity with others that exists on a subatomic level where the apparent space separating persons is revealed as an unbroken continuum. Heightened empathy in individuals derives from an enhanced power of their sensors, so to speak, within this continuum. Persons lacking empathy are those with broken, or destroyed, sensors. It is out of such empathy-driven "units of action" that the desire for "constructive nonconformity" comes. We are at our roots, far from the destructive, anarchist and anarcho-hedonist forms of non-conformity, whose "units of action" are animated by anger and negativity. But dominant culture has defined us in those terms, as being within that camp, because in fact, the Dionysian anarchist paradigm is nothing more than the flip side of conformist male-dominated society.

The pure anarchist, the likes of David Graeber, an anthropology professor at the University of London who's a key organizer of the 2011 "Occupy Wall Street" movement, proposes an individualist defiance of norms that is, at its core, no different than the asocial actions of the greed-driven Wall Street scions he opposes. The self-centered "units of action" are identical, which is why the paragons of our culture have no problem with angry anarchists. They are cut from the same cloth. In fact, it has been a long-standing form of counterinsurgency against genuine civil rights and labor movements for constructive reform to unleash anarchist elements upon them to confuse and misdirect them.

That's what happened to the gay liberation movement in the period after Stonewall. Fueled by the civil rights movement of the 1960s, the gay movement was swiftly co-opted by an anarcho-hedonist, "sex, drugs and rock and roll" counterculture that dissembled the movement and turned it into a mandate for engaging in the kind of massively excessive impersonal sex that led to AIDS. Gays were swept under the convenient umbrella of Dionysian anarchy, a form of "rebellion" over which the prevailing forces in straight male-dominated culture have had complete containment and control. That became our "brand," so to speak. I propose it is time to "re-brand" ourselves as Prometheans, not Dionysians. It is both accurate and necessary.

As Promethean givers of life and love, consider the impact on the overall society in the U.S. that 400,000 of us – 400,000 Prometheans – were wiped out by AIDS before beginning to fulfill their potentials and contributions. Many of our society's current problems stem from this gaping absence. We are challenged to reclaim our proper role at every level from the bottom to the top of our society to rekindle the Promethean fire.

The unprecedented claim I make – that gay identity is best associated with the ancient Greek myth of Prometheus, a "third way" distinct from the dual options of Apollonian law or Dionysian hedonism in the German philosopher Nietzsche's system – could not have been made in all of history before now, before Stonewall, when the fullest realization of the implications of an open, affirming gay identity has become possible for the first time. History indicates there were similar circumstances in ancient Greece, when the Prometheus myth developed, and Aeschylus wrote *Prometheus Bound*. That was when gay identity, if not hegemonic in that culture, was nearly so. It has not been that way since, especially not in the context of a rising civilization steeped in profound thought, as opposed to something dying and degenerate, like Rome's latter days.

In the European Renaissance, moral reference points were attached to Judeo-Christian imagery, thus it was the Old Testament David, the psalmist, slayer of Goliath and just ruler, whose love for Jonathan was famous, that became the symbol for a noble (gay) identity.

But appreciation of Prometheus, the Titan who stole fire from Zeus and, along with knowledge and reason, gave it to man, was held back because Prometheus was too Christ-like and thereby posed a threat to the authority of church. Like Christ, Prometheus came down to offer great gifts to man, and for doing so was punished by Zeus and caused to suffer for eternity, tied to a stone as an eagle ate out his liver every day. Therefore, characterizations of Prometheus have been skewed.

As we saw earlier, in *Prometheus, Archetypal Image of Human Existence*, (1944) Carl Kerenyi wrote *Prometheus and Christ* were incompatible concepts because Prometheus remained a Titan while Christ became "fully man." The German poet Johann W. von Goethe wrote a definitive poem about Prometheus in 1772, defining him as a defiant rebel, railing against the tyranny of Zeus. That image became prevalent, some equating him with the ultimate rebel against God, Satan in John Milton's *Paradise Lost*. Because he gave man fire and invention, Prometheus was also assailed for unleashing man's arrogance over nature. These characterizations are terribly flawed because they misrepresent what, at his core, motivated Prometheus. He stood against the arbitrary authority of Zeus on behalf of man's weal, giving mankind fire, the fire of the human spirit, and the tools for his advance and liberation from want, ignorance and pain. His "impulse tendency" being love, it is enacted by a resolute determination to provide that spiritual fire. Love and fire are thus one, and they trace their origins to the corners of, and to the origin of, the universe, itself. Love and fire united for the "Big Bang" that got it all started. (That's my Big Bang Theory. I love you, Sheldon!)

Reductionist treatments of the issue, such as *The Man Jesus Loved: Homoerotic Narratives from the New Testament* (2003) by Theodore W. Jennings Jr. miss the most basic point. Same sex love is not discovered by picking through scriptures for evidence of explicitly gay behavior.

It cries out from the totality of the passionate Promethean love that Christ was, in his parables, prayers and Sermon on the Mount, for unqualified love in defiance of authority, and for love suffering on a cross.

THE NATURAL ROLE OF GAY PEOPLE

IT HAS BEEN MY EFFORT THROUGH my "Gay Science" to cause some phalanx of gay people to take seriously what the natural role of gay people within the wider society means for us. The gifts homosexuals bring, taken as a whole through history, include natural propensities toward heightened sensibility, alternate perspectives and constructive nonconformity. They lead us to constantly strive for the transformation of social orders toward justice, compassion and progress.

We cannot be content with our own so-called "equality." Equality with what? Equality in a society that is as unequal as ours requires far more than equal rights laws for homosexuals, alone.

Those laws will come. But in a society where the average income of the top one percent is $1.4 million a year, and for the remaining 99 percent is $30,000 per year, there is a structural inequality that will take enormous courage, and the full exercise of our collective creative power, to set right. A new, menacing wave of hateful reaction is rising to not only threaten us, but women, workers and immigrants, as well.

Equality? Gay people historically have stood staunchly for the enfranchisement of all persons. We demand and claim our enfranchisement only to empower us to extend that claim universally. African-Americans in our society received full equality under the law over 50 years ago. Do they feel equal, in fact, today? Smug, comfortably self-indulgent, apathetic cynicism are symptoms of a suffocated gay soul. The hopelessly jaded homosexual is a sad sight to see, a visible setback to the aspirations of humanity as a whole. We will never be "equal" in the sense of some hypothetical societal equilibrium. We will never be "equal," except in an inadequate legal sense, because we are not "equal" with the prevailing structures and mores of a brutal, straight-male dominated society. We should be deeply thankful for that. "Equality" and "liberation" are two fundamentally different things. Liberation is our biggest challenge.

Thanks to a swift intervention by GLAAD, a PBS commentator quickly apologized for allowing bigoted comments on his show by a leader of the Family Forum that associated heinous child rape at Penn State with the issue of gay adoptions. Our gay sensibility – a gay self-identity and new morality that are the focus of this series – is the polar opposite to the abuse charged in that case, which is similar to patterns of what has likely been eons of abuse in the Catholic Church. Our identity is rooted in our heightened empathy, especially for women and children. Clearly, anyone with that attribute cannot tolerate the kind of cruel rape that is perpetrated by authoritative adults against helpless children, whose psyches are often shattered and crippled for life as a result.

Empathy and compassion have to be stripped away, if there in the first place, from the souls of any who become consumed by the ravenous and perverse passions that fuel relentless abuse.

Throughout history, since the time of Socrates and Plato, the special role in the natural order of creation that homosexuals play involves standing against the excessive abuses of straight male dominion in defense of women and children. We form the buffer that resists the brutality associated with unbridled rape-like behaviors of male supremacist practitioners. We set up institutions grounded in notions of virtue and compassion to not only protect, but to advance the self-empowerment of the downtrodden.

Index

of Proper names, Book and Film titles, and Keywords

A

Adair, Gilbert 87

Adler, Alfred 174

Aiken, Clay 43

Albee, Edward 42

Aldrich, Robert 44

Alexander Hamilton 33

Alexander, Ross 63

A Nation in Crisis and the Rise of the American Right 90

A Natural History of Homosexuality 44

And the Band Played On 163

Angels in America 71

Anthony, Susan B. 45

A Streetcar Named Desire 62

Atherton, Gertrude 34

Auden, W. H. 42

Augustine, St. 73, 84, 101, 102, 103

B

Bachardy, Don 15

Bagemihl, Bruce 80

Bale, Christian 188

Ball, Lucille 15

Barrie, J.M. 14

Beard, James 42

Beasley, Maurine H. 90

Before Wilde: Sex Between Men in Britain's Age of Reform 79

Behind the Mask of the Mattachine 80

Bell, Jamie 187

Bennett, Alan 185

Berkeley Barb 44

Berkeley Tribe 44

Berlandt, Konstantin 119

Berlin Stories 62

Bernstein, Leonard 42

Billy Elliot 186

Biological Exuberance: Animal Homosexuality and Natural Diversity 80

Blank, Hanne 79

Bogarde, Dirk 43, 63

Borrowed Time 103

Boswell, John 44

Bowie, David 43, 188

Boyd, Nan Alamilla 29

Boy George 43

Bram, Christopher 119

Brands, H. W. 89

Britten, Benjamin 185

Burr, Aaron 34

Burroughs, Augusten 42

Burroughs, William 58

Burr, Raymond 43

C

Cabaret 15, 62

Capote, Truman 42

Captain Blood 63

Carpenter, Edward 45

Cat on a Hot Tin Roof 130

Chamberlain, Richard 43

Chernow, Ron 33

Chibbaro, Lou 163

Christopher and His Kind 62

City of God 73

Clairborne, Craig 42

Clay, Henry 35

Clift, Montgomery 42

Cohn, Roy 199

Cole Porter 31

Common Sense 141

Compton, Louis 44

Compton's Cafeteria riot 97

Conceived in the Shadow of Tennessee Williams 120

Connery, Sean 103

Conversations With Tennessee Williams 117

Corydon 203

Coward, Noel 42

Crane, Hart 70

Crawford, Joan 15

Crimmins, Cathy 42

Crowley, Mart 97, 125, 126

Cukor, George 43

D

Daniels, Josephus 89

Dansky, Steven F. 136

Darwin, Charles 154

Daughters of Bilitis 74

David 31

David Frost 62

Davies, Ray 43

Davis, Bette 15

Davis, Nancy 109

Dead Poets Society 93

Dean, James 15, 43

Death in Venice 61

de Havilland, Olivia 63

Democratic Enlightenment 78, 171

Denton, Sally 90

De Profundis 106

Derickson, Capt. David 35

Devlin, Albert J. 117

Diaries Volume One 126

DiCaprio, Leonardo 93

Dickens, Charles 96

Diderot, Denis 78

Diotima 67

Donatello 32

Don Carlos 78

Douglas, Alfred 61

Dover, K.D. 64

Dover, K. J. 44

Duberman, Martin 44

E

Eco, Umberto 103

Eleanor Roosevelt: Transformative First Lady 90

Electric Kool Aid Acid Test 76

Ellsworth, Col. Elmer 35

Eminent Outlaws: The Gay Writers Who Changed America 119

Erasmus 84

Eros and Civilization 73

Evolution's Rainbow: Diversity, Gender, and Sexuality in Nature and People 81

F

Faggots 60

Federalist Papers 33

Fierstein, Harvey 42

Flynn, Errol 63

Forbes, Malcolm 42

Forster, E. M. 45

Foucault, Michel 25, 88, 89, 94, 118, 151, 160, 170–172, 193, 194

Frank, Barney 42

Franklin, Benjamin 149

Frankl, Viktor 173

Freud, Sigmund 89

Friends of Dorothy 15

G

Ganymede 63

Garland, Judy 15, 147

Garrison, Daniel H. 44

Gay American History 44

Gay cancer. 138

Gay is Good 108

Gay Life and Culture: A World History 44

Gay New York 29

Gay Pioneers 107

Gay Science 166

Gay Soul: Finding the Heart of Gay Spirit and Nature 103

Gay Sunshine 44

George Chauncey 29

George III 34

Germanotta, Stefani 186

Gide, Andre 203

Gielgud, John 43

Ginsberg, Allen 59

Gittings, Barbara 107

Goeth, Johann Wolfgang von 78

Goldhaber, Maurice 72

Goodbye to Berlin 62, 131

Gosling, Ryan 161

Graeber, David 209

Grant, Cary 43

Grauerholz, James 117

"Greed is Good" 152

Greek Homosexuality 44, 64

Greene, Billy 35

Grindr 99

Guerriero, Patrick 163

Gumm, Frances Ethel 147

H

Hall, Lee 186

Halperin, David 193

Hamilton, Alexander 33

Hammarskjold, Dag 100

Hay, Harry 74

Haynes, Todd 43

Heard, Gerald 80

Helms, Richard 75

Hepburn, Katharine 15

Herman, Jerry 42

Hickok, Lorena 90

Hidden from History: Reclaiming the Gay and Lesbian Past 44

Hilter, Adolph 73

Hirschfeld, Mangus 45

Hirshman, Linda 162

Histoire Philosophique 78

History of Ancient Art 78

Hoerner, Griff 121

Homosexuality and Civilization 44

Homosexuality in Greece and Rome 44

Homosexuality in History 44

Hoover, Herbert 74

Horne, Ken 156

Hoult, Nicholas 122

How the Homosexuals Saved Civilization 42

How to Be Gay 193

Hubbard, Thomas 44

Hudson, Rock 15, 43

Hughes, Willie 54

I

I Am a Camera 62

Ibn Sina 180

"I Have a Dream" 152

Inge, William 42, 122

In Masks Outrageous and Austere 119

Isherwood, Christopher 15

Israel, Jonathan I. 78, 171

J

Jefferson, Thomas 77

Jennings Jr., Theodore W. 212

John, Elton 42

Johnson, David K. 108

Johnson, Toby 11

Jonathan 31

K

Kameny, Frank 40, 107–109, 114, 118

Katz, Jonathan 44

Kazan, Elia 122

Kennedy, Bobby 16

Kenneth Chang 72

Kerenyi, Carl 203

Kesey, Ken 75

Keynes, John Maynard 100

Kin and Kind: A Fight About the Genetics of Altruism 81

King Jr., Rev. Martin Luther 16, 16–18, 34, 39, 40, 84, 107–109, 135, 140, 148, 150, 152, 181

Kinsey Report 14

Kirk, Tommy 15

Krafft-Ebing, Richard von 79

Kramer, Larry 60, 61, 71, 100, 115, 119, 156, 169, 173

Kressley, Carson 42

Kushner, Harold S. 174

Kushner, Tony 42, 71

Kuzniar, Alice A. 78

L

Ladies of Courage 90

Lady Gaga 186

Lane, Nathan 42

Laughton, Charles 43

Laurens, John 33

Laurents, Arthur 42

Lawrence, D.H. 60

Leary, Timothy 75

Leaves of Grass 27–29, 49, 105

Lehrer, Jonah 81

Leibniz, Gottfried Wilhelm 85

Leyland, Winston 119

Liberace 13

Life *magazine* 147

Limbaug, Rush 79

Linardi, Vittorio 44

Lincoln, Abraham 34

Little Richard 43

Lorca 100

Lynde, Paul 42

M

Manhunt 99

Man's Search for Meaning 173

Marcuse, Herbert 73

Mathis, Johnny 15

Mattachine Society 74

Maurice 62

McGreevey, James 156

McGregor, Ewan 188

McKellen, Ian 43

McKenna, Neil 184

McNally, Terrence 42

Mecca, Tommi Avicolli 136

Memoirs 127

Men in Love: Homosexualities from Ganymede to Batman 44

Mercury, Freddie 42

Merrill, George 48

Meyers, Jonathan Rhys 188

Michael, George 42

Michelangelo 32

Milton, John 211

Mineo, Sal 15, 43

Mizrahi, Isaac 43

Moes, Wladyslaw 87

Mondimore, Francis Mark 44

Monette, Paul 9

Monroe, Marilyn 15

Moverman, Owen 188

Mussolini, Benito 88

My Dear Boy: Gay Love Letters Through the Centuries 53

N

Neddermeyer, Heinz 128

New York Times Magazine 15

Nichols, Mike 199

Nietzsche, Friedrich 88

Norton, Rictor 53

Notebooks 120

O

Ode: Imitations of Immortality 124

Old Yeller 15

Oliver Twist 96

On Becoming 103

Outing Goethe and His Age 78

P

Pacino, Al 199

Paine, Thomas 141

Paradise Lost 211

Parker, Mary-Louise 199

Paul 31

Perkins, Anthony 43

Peter Pan 14

Phaedrus 20

Philo 180

Picnic 123

Plato 20

Power, Tyrone 43

Prometheus and Christ 211

Prometheus: Archetypal Image of Human Existence 203

Psychopathia Sexualis 79

Q

Queers in History 44

R

Rankin, Jim 135

Raynal, A. G. 78

Recollections of Early Childhood 124

Reflections Concerning the Imitation of the Greeks 78

Regeneration 161

Reilly, Charles Nelson 43

Researches Into the Riddle of Love Between Men 45

Robbins, Jerome 42

Rockwell, Norman 13

Roosevelt, Eleanor 25, 26, 36, 37, 56, 89, 90, 95, 168, 204

Roosevelt, Franklin D. 36

Roughgarden, Joan 81

Rove, Karl 164

Russell, Paul 44

S

Sacks, Jonathan 175

Saddik, Annette 123

Saint Foucault 193

San Francisco Kalendar 44

Sargent, Dick 43

Saturday Evening Post 13

Schiller, Friedrich 78

Science and the Search for Meaning 175

Sears, James T. 80

Sedaris, David 42

Sexual Culture in Ancient Greece 44

Shakespeare, William 53

Shilts, Randy 163

Slater, Christian 103

Small Craft Warnings 62, 123

Smash the Church 136

Smash the State! The Early Years of Gay Liberation 136

Smith, Bill 164

Social Tolerance, Christianity and Homosexuality 44

Socrates 20

Sodom and Gomorrah 31

Something Cloudy, Something Clear 94

Sondheim, Stephen 42

Speed, Joshua 35

Spencer, Colin 44

Splendor in the Grass 122

Stars in My Eyes 191

States of Desire 104

Stein, Gertrude 45

Stern, Kenneth 44

Stirner, Max 88

Stonewall Riots 16, 51, 146, 148, 149, 155

Straight, the Surprisingly Short History of Heterosexuality 79

Streep, Meryl 199

Suddenly Last Summer 14, 69

Sullivan, Harry Stack 100

Swartz, Mimi 15

T

Tab Hunter 15

Taylor, Rip 43

Tchaikovsky, Peter 42

Teal, Don 119

The Age of Reason 143

The Birdcage 25

The Birth of Tragedy 202

The Boys in the Band 97

The Broken Tower 130

The Children's Hour 63

The Confession 156

The Conqueror: Being the True and Romantic Story of Alexander Hamilton 34

The Council on Religion and the Homosexual 95

The Dancing Boys of Afghanistan 53

The Effeminist 44

The Ego and His Own: The Case of the Individual Against Authority 88

The Gay 100 44

The Gay Militants 119

The Great Partnership: God, Science and the Search for Meaning 175

The Habit of Art 185

The History Boys 185

The Intermediate Sex 45

The Last of Mr. Norris 132

The Lavender Scare: The Cold War Persecution of Gays and Lesbians in the Federal Government 108

The Lost 131

The Man Jesus Loved: Homoerotic Narratives from the New Testament 212

The Myth of the Modern Homosexual 94

The Name of the Rose 103

The Normal Heart 100

The Picture of Dorian Gray 95

The Plots Against the President: FDR 90

The Real Tadzio: Thomas Mann's Death in Venice and the Boy Who Inspired It 87

The Republic 143

The Secret Life of Oscar Wilde 184

The Symposium 20

The Wizard of Oz 15, 147

This Boy's Life 93

Thomas, Norman 74

Thompson, Emma 199

Thompson, Mark 103

Townsend, Pete 43

Traitor to His Class: the Privileged Life and Radical Presidency of Franklin Delano Roosevelt 89

Tripp, C. A. 35

Tyrwhitt, Thomas 54

U

Ulrichs, Karl Heinrich 45

Upchurch, Charles 79

V

Valentino, Rudolph 43

Velvet Goldmine 187

Verrocchio 32

Vicinis, Martha 44

Victim 63

Victory: The Triumphant Gay Revolution 162

Vidal, Gore 42

Vieux Carre 94

Village People 43

Village Voice 58, 117

Vincenz, Lilli 40

von Goethe, Johann W. 211

W

Wainwright, Rufus 42

Wallace, Henry A. 74

Warhol, Andy 43

Washington Blade 163

Washington, George 33

Waters, John 42

Weir, Johnny 25

Weir, Peter 93

Welcome to My World 191

Whale, James 43

White, Edmund 104

Whitman, Walt 27–31, 34, 35, 37,
    44, 45, 48, 49, 61, 70, 100, 105,
    204

*Wide Open Town: A History of
    Queer San Francisco to 1965* 29

Wilde, Oscar 31, 54, 61, 95–96,
    106, 180–184, 187, 192

Wilder, Thornton 42

Williams, Tennessee 14, 31, 42,
    44, 45, 56–62, 69, 70–71, 74,
    94–95, 98, 100, 117–131, 158

Wilson, E. O. 81

Wilson, Lanford 42

Wilson, Patrick 199

Winckelmann, Johann Joachim
    78

Wolff, Tobias 93

Wollstonecraft, Mary 45

Women in Love 60

Y

York, Michael 43

Z

Zeffirelli, Franco 43

Zeus 63

About the Author

Nicholas F. (Nick) Benton was an honor graduate of the Pacific School of Religion in 1969 and co-founder of the Berkeley Gay Liberation Front in 1970. In 1991, he founded the weekly *Falls Church News-Press* (www.fcnp.com) in the northern Virginia suburbs of Washington, D.C. and after 28 years it is widely recognized as the most progressive newspaper in Virginia. As its openly gay owner and editor, Benton has served twice as president of the local Chamber of Commerce, been named Falls Church's "Pillar of the Community" twice and "Business Person of the Year" once, and had his newspaper named "Business of the Year" twice.

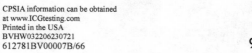